The Lower Fal

IN OLD PHOTOGRAPHS

In the Middle Ages the inland towns of the Fal estuary assumed jurisdiction over its waters and Truro claimed all but the Penryn river. This was confirmed by Royal Charter in 1589 when the mayor of Truro also became Mayor of Falmouth (which in those days meant Carrick Roads as far south as Black Rock). After the town of Falmouth obtained its Charter in 1661, Truro Corporation continued to assert its ancient rights and in 1709 perambulated the bounds as far as Black Rock. This provocative act resulted in a lawsuit which created a new southern limit to Truro's jurisdiction between Tarra (now Penarrow) Point and Messack Point on the northern shore of St Just creek. Granite pillars were later erected at each side inscribed with the letters 'T.B.', interpreted as either 'Truro Borough' or 'Truro Boundary'. In the picture above one of the several formal ceremonies of 'beating the bounds' is seen taking place in 1878 with the mayor of Truro, Thomas Chirgwin, escorted by his mace-bearers and members of the Corporation. The same limit is used as the boundary for this book: the estuary north of this line will be included in a companion volume on the upper Fal estuary.

The Lower Fal

IN OLD PHOTOGRAPHS

Collected by PETER GILSON

ALAN SUTTON

Alan Sutton Publishing Limited
Phoenix Mill · Far Thrupp
Stroud · Gloucestershire

First Published 1992

Copyright © Peter Gilson 1992

British Library Cataloguing
in Publication Data

Gilson, Peter
Lower Fal in Old Photographs
I. Title
942 . 378

ISBN 0–7509–0024–5

Typeset in 9/10 Sabon.
Typsetting and origination by
Alan Sutton Publishing Limited.
Printed in Great Britain by
WBC Print Ltd, Bridgend.

Contents

Introduction

The tidal water that comprises the estuary of the River Fal consists of the large central area of Carrick Roads from which branch a number of tidal creeks. The central one leads north to Truro and comprises the lower part of the River Fal and its tributary the Truro River. On the west side the lower tidal section of the Penryn river is often called the Inner Harbour, and gives the large anchorage off the town of Falmouth. The lower creeks dry out to an expanse of mud at low tide but fill to form beautiful expanses of water when the tide is high.

Winding north in Carrick Roads and extending through the narrow King Harry Reach as far as Tolverne is a very deep channel which, at high spring tides, contains over 38m (120 ft) of water off St Anthony lighthouse and 17m (50 ft) off Tolverne, 8 km from the open sea. This great depth of water results from variations in sea level over the last million years associated with the Ice Age, in reality four cold 'glacial' periods separated by warmer 'inter-glacials'. During the glacials ice covered much of the land in northern Europe for tens of thousands of years, which could only have originated in the sea, and sea level dropped by as much as 200 ft – imagine standing on Falmouth's sea-front and looking south with no sea in sight! This expanse of exposed sea floor was covered at times when the climate was getting warmer with small trees, today's 'submerged forests', visible on rare occasions at Maenporth, Praa Sands and Mount's Bay. It was during these periods that deep channels were eroded by melt-water flowing from the ice towards the lower sea level. The melting of land ice during the warm inter-glacials caused sea levels to rise, and in one of these, when the climate was warmer than it is today, the sea level rose higher than it is at present creating a feature seen along several parts of the south Cornish coast – the remains of former beaches up to twelve feet above their present level. Good examples of raised beaches may be seen at Sunnycove, Newporth, near Maenporth and at Pendower. The most recent rise in sea level filled the pre-existing river valleys to form the present deep, branching inlets known as rias or drowned valleys, other examples of which may be seen in the estuaries at Helford, Fowey, Looe, the Tamar, Salcombe and Dartmouth. It is impossible to date geological events with any great precision but the final rise in sea level which created the Fal ria began between six and seven thousand years ago. Geologically, this is very recent, especially when compared with the age of the rocks through which the estuary runs. The clay-shales of Devonian age, known locally as 'killas', are, very approximately, 400 million years old.

Archaeological remains around the estuary are sparse. An Iron Age fort was probably destroyed in the building of Pendennis Castle while, further inland, prehistoric settlement sites have been identified at Roundwood, Golden and Carvossa although their ages are uncertain. Roundwood is sited near the junction of the Fal and Truro rivers; the other two were at one time easily accessible via the tidal creek stretching up to Tregony, until mineral waste silted up the creek from the seventeenth century onwards. Greater details of these and most other archaeological sites in Cornwall may be found in Craig Weatherhill's fascinating book *Cornovia*.

The older towns on the estuary, such as Penryn, Truro and Tregony, were also built inland, away from the coast because of the risk of attack from the sea. The name 'Falmouth' had long been used for the lower part of the harbour and the only signs of settlement on the present town site up to the early seventeenth century were at Arwenack, the Killigrew Manor House, and a poor collection of inns and fishermen's cottages around the small creek at Smithick, where the Market Strand and Prince of Wales' Pier stand today. King Henry VIII had Castles built at many strategic points around the coast, including those at Pendennis and St Mawes, to counter the threat of attack by his continental enemies, and a wonderful description of these early days is given in Winston Graham's *The Grove of Eagles*. Penzance, Newlyn and Mousehole were attacked by Spanish ships in 1589 and it is believed that the Spanish, following the failure of their first Armada, planned to invade England by capturing a sheltered harbour, possibly the Fal, and using it as a bridgehead. Although never called upon to resist a Spanish attack, the castles did at least provide the necessary defence at the harbour entrance to enable the town to grow up near the open sea. The only serious military activity seen at Pendennis was during the Civil War, when Cromwell's army laid siege to the Castle for 153 days after which the Royalists were forced to surrender – under remarkably favourable terms. After the surrender the town began to grow, as tradesmen and merchants came in to supply the varying needs of the 'occupying' army, so when Killigrew control was re-established after the Restoration and the Borough Charter was granted in 1661 there began a power struggle between the merchants who formed the Corporation and the Manor which was to last for over a century and ended only with the departure of the Killigrew successors.

In 1688 Falmouth was established as the principal port for the Post Office Packet Service, first for the Spanish mail, which could not travel by land because of war in Europe, and at its peak in the early years of the nineteenth century to many Iberian, trans-Atlantic, Caribbean and Mediterranean destinations. Falmouth was chosen for three reasons: sailing ships could enter and leave the harbour at all stages of the tide, by day or night and in nearly all weathers; it gave almost direct access to the Atlantic without having to sail down-Channel into the prevailing westerly winds, and there was less danger of attack by foreign ships than in the narrow confines of the English Channel further east. This was a prosperous time for Falmouth and one of the several benefits which the packets brought to the growing town was the introduction of tourists. As the packets carried passengers who would arrive in the town after what was often a harrowing journey by stage-coach or by coastal vessel, a few days recuperation was needed before embarking on another equally daunting voyage. After 1815 local publishers and booksellers, never slow to grasp such an opportunity, produced guide books and 'histories' of the town and vicinity which must have been as useful to these early visitors as they are valuable to present-day historians and researchers as they paint a delightful picture of the Fal estuary, its attractions and activities, nearly two centuries ago. By the time steamships finally replaced the sailing packets in 1850, when the Post Office used existing shipping companies to carry the mail from Southampton and Liverpool which had railway links with London, the future of Falmouth was (within fifteen years) assured by the arrival of the railway, the building of the Docks and the construction of the first purpose-built 'tourist' hotel on the sea-front – all in the 1860s. The new-look Falmouth became busy and prosperous as a ship-building and repairing port, pilotage centre, commercial entrepot – bulk commodities were conveyed by water as far as possible up each creek before transfer to land transport – and as the first landfall for the large windjammers, survivors of sail despite the arrival of steam, who came to the port from all over the world 'For Orders'. The ancient Borough of Penryn was not intimidated by the growth of its upstart neighbour and, despite the problems of silting in its river, specialized in such activities as the cattle trade, fertilizer processing, paper manufacture, specialist foundry work and, above all, the granite industry.

Social changes aided by GWR advertising brought ever-increasing numbers of holiday-makers to share the many attractions of the estuary towards the end of the nineteenth century, giving rise to a hybrid variety of steamer, the passenger-tug, and Falmouth's waterfront slowly changed to cater more and more for the visitor. For a time Falmouth and Flushing attracted invalids by emphasizing their climatic advantages but simultaneous reports into the health of the Borough, blaming poor quality water and inadequate sewage disposal for epidemics of enteric disease, tended to discourage such visitors. And so, today, Falmouth's magnificent harbour is used as both working port and anchorage as well as a popular recreational area for all branches of water-sports and sightseeing.

References to *Falmouth* in the captions refer to additional information in *Falmouth in Old Photographs*, published by Alan Sutton in 1990.

SECTION ONE

The Harbour Entrance

St Anthony Lighthouse, signalling the entrance to Falmouth harbour and backed here by a patch of woodland, was erected by local builders Olver and Sons in 1834–5 at a cost of £2,895 and an extra £980 for 'ancillary structures'. Safe though Falmouth harbour is, its entrance is not easy to locate on a dark and stormy night and the decision to build it was the result of a disastrous storm in the autumn of 1833. After a fine, breezy day which tempted several vessels to leave Plymouth, a strong south-easterly gale blew up, catching these and other ships on a lee shore on a moonless night. Ten were wrecked between Dodman Point and the Lizard and it was agreed that a lighthouse showing the position of the harbour would have enabled many of them to gain the safety of Falmouth's sheltered waters, where at other times over five hundred vessels had lain in perfect safety. In addition to its bright light, the lighthouse was equipped in 1882 with the two-ton fog bell seen here. The local newspaper reported: 'It was landed on the rocks by the steamer *Resolute*: a pair of wooden shears having been erected on top of the tower, the immense mass of metal was raised by means of a hand winch and a system of double pulleys and bolted to the main beam from which it is to be suspended.' In 1954 the bell was replaced by an electric fog-warning apparatus. (See *Falmouth* p. 123).

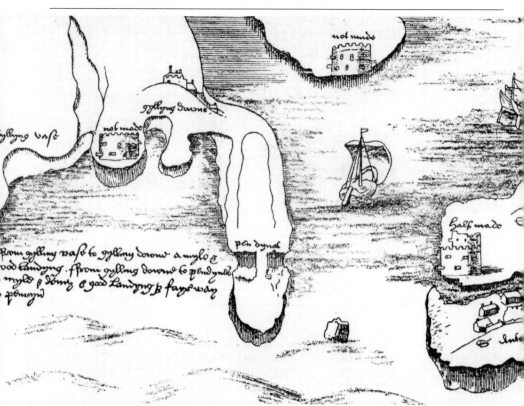

This extract from a 1539 map known as the 'Great Map of the West' shows the harbour entrance with the castles proposed by Henry VIII to guard against the threat of an invasion. The need for some form of defence had been shown in 1537 when French and Spanish warships had sailed unopposed into the harbour and fought a battle which took both fleets upstream nearly as far as Malpas. The defences on Trefusis Point and Swanpool Point (both marked here as 'not made') were never to be built. St Mawes is marked 'half made' and the inscription on Pendennis Point (Pen Dynas on the map, meaning 'castle headland') suggests that a defensive work of some kind occupied the headland before the present castle was built. The absence of any contemporary design on Pen Dynas is not easy to explain but, whatever the reason, plans must have changed rapidly as the castle was begun in 1540. Apart from the castles, villages are shown at St Anthony and St Mawes, but Falmouth is non-existent, the only habitation being Arwenack, over the hill from Gyllyngdune.

Black Rock, covered by 9 ft of water at high spring tide but having a low spring tide exposure of approximately 200 ft by 100 ft, stands just east of the centre of the harbour entrance but considering its position, surprisingly few vessels have gone ashore on it (see *Falmouth* p. 119). The earliest known marker, an elm pole set in lead, was erected by an early rector of Falmouth who was then able to claim sixpence from every vessel entering the harbour, although he encountered some difficulty in collecting his money. In 1813 it was considered as a possible site for a lighthouse, but in 1837 a granite column designed by the Trinity Board was erected by Olver and Sons at a cost of £2,260 9s. 10d.: the top of the rock was levelled to form a base 20 ft square and the 37 ft high conical structure shown above was set 6 ft into the rock. The mast on the top was 25 ft high and topped by a ribbed copper sphere 6 ft in diameter to which steps led from the base of the cone and in which, it is said, three men could shelter from storm until rescued. Tide and weather delayed its completion until 1840. In March 1858 the *Northern Empire*, a 1,500-ton sailing vessel of Oldenburg, with a cargo of 2,400 tons of guano, was anchored outside the harbour entrance to enable the captain to make a quick getaway on receipt of his orders. It was not a safe anchorage for the time of year – the pilot was suspended for placing the vessel in such a dangerous situation – and a sudden equinoctial gale blew up. One of her two anchors had fouled and a harbour tug which tried to tow her to a safer position was unequal to the task. One of the larger Channel ferries offered assistance but the captain would not pay the fee required and allowed his vessel to drift towards the harbour on the southerly gale. Unfortunately, she struck the northern ledge of Black Rock, quickly filled, and sank with only her upper works visible at low water. The cargo was completely lost, but as the weather moderated parts of the vessel were salvaged and were on sale a week later in Trethowan's yard on the Bar, including a 93 ft mainmast, a 72 ft foremast and 40 ft bowsprit. During a strong October gale twenty-two years later, the Whitby brig *Marys*, with a cargo of salt from Runcorn to Newcastle, ran on to Black Rock and began to break up. The crew of six took to the lifeboat but heavy seas swamped it and the men were struggling in the water. The harbourmaster, Captain Richard Sherris, was able to pick up the captain in his steam launch, while the mate of the *Berkshire*, at anchor nearby, saved two others. The cook, an able seaman and a boy were lost. A week later the tug *Kimberley* towed off the remains of the hull as it was a danger to navigation. Within a fortnight three bodies were picked up in various parts of the harbour, and a few weeks later Capt. Sherris was presented with a Certificate of Thanks from the NLI by the town mayor, Mr J.C. Downing, and the *Berkshire*'s mate, Mr Hatch, was awarded the Institution's Silver Medal.

In this print drawn and engraved by the brothers Samuel and Nathaniel Buck in 1734 to match a similar print of Pendennis Castle drawn at the same time, St Mawes Castle stands on the northern entrance of its creek (see *Falmouth* p. 12). Built simultaneously beween 1540 and 1545, the two fortresses were part of the coastal defences of Henry VIII against the threat of invasion first from the sea and, later, in the reign of Elizabeth I, from the land. Apart from their defensive role, the Castle garrisons fulfilled other tasks, one of which was to collect tolls from vessels entering the harbour. In 1630 the Deputy Governor of St Mawes, Captain Hannibal Bonython, was accused by the Killigrews of stopping and searching ships, a practice 'which had been accustomed to be done at Pendennis only'. A typical British compromise was reached whereby vessels west of Black Rock should be dealt with by Pendennis while those to the east should be the responsibility of St Mawes. This same Hannibal Bonython, promoted to Major and made Castle Governor, survived complaints of smuggling, embezzlement of soldiers' pay and, worst of all, 'disaffection to the King's cause' only to deliver the Castle to the Roundhead General Sir Thomas Fairfax in 1646 without firing a shot. The Castle retained its governor until April 1842 when the office was abolished and the senior artillery officer assumed control over the establishment. By this time the two garrisons were manned largely by militia units, with a core of regular soldiers for administration and instruction. From as early as 1609 the Castle and its soldiers suffered periods of neglect by the Crown only to be fortified in times of national emergency. In 1854 the *West Briton* reported that, because of the Russian War, 'Several

large pieces of ordnance have lately been landed here and soldiers employed in conveying them to the Castle.' Newspaper reports in peace-time were in a somewhat different vein and a criticism of December 1884 was that, 'This castle is manned by two gunners of the RA and it is said that they receive their pay weekly from Pendennis. To convey it across to them the garrison boat, with six men and a coxswain, is employed, the men being paid 4d. each and the coxswain 6d. every week for this duty . . . for what could be done as well by one man crossing in the St Mawes steamer at 28s. 2d. per annum, or by post office order at half that amount!' As the nature of both naval craft and defensive artillery changed in the second half of the nineteenth century, the harbour's strategic requirements necessitated the establishment of gun positions further south on St Anthony Head. At first, in 1885, the new defences were armed with 64-pounder muzzle-loaders manned by the Royal Miners Artillery, but as the new iron-clad warships were armour plated such guns proved useless and new, breech-loading 6-inch guns with greater range and using armour-piercing shells were installed in emplacements facing the open sea. Through two world wars these batteries were manned by members of the local Territorial Army units. The guns were kept in operative condition up to 1955 and units from all over the country came here for firing training, but in 1956 Coast Artillery was pronounced obsolete and within two years the large guns were removed. In 1959 the buildings on the site were converted into holiday accommodation by the National Trust who also operate the adjacent car park in what must be one of the finest locations in Britain.

Above, an early twentieth-century postcard by Bragg shows the passenger-tug *Roseland* of the St Mawes Steam Tug and Passenger Company Ltd leaving St Mawes quay. *Roseland* was built and engined at the Cox and Company yard next to Falmouth Docks and operated the ferry service between Falmouth and St Mawes for sixty years until honourably retired in 1946. The fields above the ferry's bow have a notice advertising them as 'building land', and as the village grew in popularity, especially after the First World War, this land and much more further along the creek was built over so that the greatly enlarged settlement shown in the aerial photograph below extends round Polvarth Point and along the Percuil River. Here, Freshwater beach was the site of the Peters shipyard, where the famous six-oared gigs were built to take pilots from several ports in Cornwall and the Isles of Scilly to meet ships well out to sea, while others were used for salvage, as lifeboats and for smuggling. Only when Falmouth became very busy were gigs replaced by cutters, each of which carried several pilots and could stay at sea for several days.

Two views of St Mawes in the nineteenth century show many features typical of buildings of that time. Walls are built almost entirely of the soft clay shale, quarried locally and known as 'killas'. Some exterior walls are plastered but, apart from some slate-hung surfaces, the natural stone predominates. Bricks, heavy and expensive to import, appear to have been used solely for chimneys; slate, used for some walls and roofs, was imported from quarries in other parts of the county. The view above shows the alley known as Hillhead, and at one time the only way into the village, leading up to the Rising Sun inn which may have begun its life as a kiddlywink, a beer and spirit shop which relied largely on smuggled goods: the sign board on the wall above its porched doorway marks its location, with the fishermen posing below it. Below is a residential area leading up from the Victory inn, showing the way a steep hill slope was developed by arranging its housing in steps or terraces.

These two views of St Mawes harbour and waterfront show several notable differences. The older, above, shows the original fishing village clustered around the quay and consisting of whitewashed cottages, fish cellars and stores, several of them still thatched. The waterside road is obstructed by a wall, the door in which was locked at night at one time necessitating a long detour to reach the quay from the east end of the village. The more recent buildings up the hill behind the harbour and stretching into the distance towards the castle are the earliest signs of the village's gradual transition into what is now an exclusively residential, retirement and tourist settlement. In the picture below, taken about twenty years later, much of the old waterfront architecture remains, but the impact of tourism is seen with the Ship and Castle hotel, built about 1900, dominating the scene and a passenger vessel moored alongside the quay, its tarpaulin rigged to shade its passengers from the sun, or perhaps to shelter them from the rain.

The *Daisy* of Devoran is seen here at low tide unloading a bagged cargo which is being lifted into a cart on the quay above by hand, despite the presence of a nearby crane. A quay has existed here since the early sixteenth century, when Leland described the place as 'a pretty fischer town with pere'. Water transport has always been important throughout the Fal estuary and St Mawes has been especially favoured not only for its position near the harbour entrance but also because of the depth of water in its creek, said to be the result of dredging sand for agricultural fertilizer, enabling large vessels to use its quay. Fishing has always been a significant occupation. In 1826 there were ten seines operating, employing 155 men, but by 1893 there were only two, owned by Richard Collins and Horatio Step, the harbourmaster. St Mawes' position near the harbour entrance was a distinct disadvantage before the Castle was built as it was open to attack from the sea, and Breton raiders frequently landed and set part of the village ablaze. Its position was, however, an advantage later, when its pilots were better placed than their Falmouth counterparts, and in 1893 there were eighteen resident in the village. St Mawes was proclaimed a borough as early as 1562, and from that date sent two MPs to Parliament. After 1784 the whole village was owned by the Marquis of Buckingham whose sole reason for ownership was to enable him to control the two MPs from this 'rotten borough', one of ten altogether in Cornwall. After all such boroughs were disenfranchised by the Reform Act of 1832 and Municipal Corporation Act of 1835, St Mawes held no value for its patron, who put it all up for sale. The *West Briton* advertised: 'Highly important freehold properties, comprising the whole town of St Mawes . . . containing about 60 dwelling houses, the Fountain Inn, the St Mawes Arms, commodious fish cellars, numerous private residences and several acres of very eligible building land extending to St Mawes Castle.' Within twenty years the business of the village had declined to such an extent that a group of local businessmen and gentry sponsored the St Mawes Pier and Harbour Act in 1854, which gave the limits of the harbour as between Castle and Carricknath Points in the west and, in the east, Polvarth and Amsterdam Points.

The waterside village of St Mawes stood on top of a low cliff until, as *Kelly's Directory* of 1893 said, 'by the exertions and under the superintendence of the late Revd C.W. Carlyon, former rector of St Just, a sea wall with a parapet was built along the centre front of the town'. In normal times this is enough to protect the buildings behind it, but in 1872 the pier and much of the sea wall was destroyed and rebuilt a year later. In 1883 the *Penryn Advertiser* reported that recent heavy gales had destroyed much of the sea wall, which was being repaired by Olvers to a length of 350 ft and a height between 5 and 11 ft at a cost of several hundred pounds. In 1962, when these pictures were taken, a severe south-westerly gale happened to coincide with a high spring tide and, together, they created the scenes shown here.

In the aftermath of the storm seen opposite extensive damage to both sea wall and parapet was inflicted. Some buildings were severely damaged by waves, wind and the stones thrown up by the raging seas. Luckily, the pier seems to have withstood this particular onslaught.

At the head of Froe creek there was once a tide mill, the barrier for which is seen here with the mill pool on the near side and the mill house on the right. Exact dates for this are uncertain, but it is thought to have been working well into the nineteenth century as in 1809 the *Royal Cornwall Gazette* advertised for sale: 'Newbuilt dwelling house and water grist mills called Frow mills . . . worth the attention of flour dealers . . . the premises . . . desirably situated for any person wishing to embark in the coal or timber trade!' Although this last statement seems like an early example of estate agents' exaggeration, coal was occasionally unloaded here up to the early part of this century, the schooners having first 'lightened' at Percuil before entering this shallow creek at high tide. The hill slope in the foreground, separating the creek from the open sea to the east, forms part of a narrow isthmus barely two hundred yards wide along which runs the road to St Anthony Head and lighthouse.

Percuil stands at the head of navigation of St Mawes creek. Coastal schooners and ketches carried bulk cargoes up at high tide for hundreds of years before the use of petrol-driven lorries and the improvement of road surfaces following the First World War slowly replaced this ancient method of transport. Vessels would be left high and dry as the tide went out and unloaded into horse-drawn carts for carriage to Gerrans, 'capital' of the Roseland peninsula, or to any of the large number of farms in this fertile agricultural area. This 'outside' barge (above), a local term for a vessel which ventures out of the harbour into the open sea, has a cargo of what appears to be roadstone from the Lizard quarries at Porthoustock and Porthallow ready to be unloaded into carts such as the one on the road above the beach. The same procedure is taking place below, with the ketch *Hero* unloading coal down a chute into one cart while another waits patiently on the beach. Out in the creek, the passenger-tug *Roseland* has brought some form of cargo which has been rowed ashore and unloaded by the men standing by the landing stage (which is wheeled up and down depending on the state of the tide) into smaller donkey carts. The mouth of Froe creek can be seen above the steamer's funnel.

Above, another ketch unloads what is probably a cargo of guano, brought into Falmouth by windjammers from the coast of Chile and carried to creek-head sites such as this to be stored in the thatched shed at the end of the road leading from the beach. The ketch below is high and dry on the beach with several carts in attendance and the large number of sacks on the foreshore suggests that oysters are being loaded for export, probably to France. Although oyster dredging has ceased in St Mawes creek, for many centuries it was one of the most productive parts of the estuary. The small boat in the foreground is for seine fishing, the holes in the side being for oars: thole pins were not used as the nets would snag on them. Unfortunately, Percuil looks very different today: the buildings on these pages have long since disappeared and been replaced by a functional concrete monstrosity for the benefit of yachtsmen who are the creek's main users today.

Place House stands at the head of its small creek, together with the church of St Anthony, the tower of which is visible behind the centre of the house: they have been closely linked since Admiral Henry Thomas Spry was given Place by Henry VIII in the 1540s. Legend and mystery had long since surrounded the site. The myth of the Phoenician tin trade at Place has at last been dispelled and there is no proof for stories which suggest Jesus visited the 'port' as a ship's carpenter in company with his uncle, Joseph of Aramathea, or that it was the home of the old kings of Cornwall in the sixth century, but its attribution as an early monastery is more likely to be authentic. Several generations of the Spry family are commemorated on plaques in the sadly neglected St Anthony church, and several of these have had close connections with the Royal Navy. The best known dates from the mid-eighteenth century. In 1744 Richard Spry took command of the *Comet* on the West Indies station and was captured a year later by a Spanish privateer but managed to escape. He was in command of the *Chester* frigate in 1746, and in 1748 he joined another Cornishman, Admiral Boscawen, on blockading duties in the East Indies and, later, off the coast of India. By 1753 he was back in home waters and, in *Garland*, was active on preventive duties around the Cornish coast, where his encounters with smugglers in Gerrans Bay would have proved interesting. Promotion followed and his duties took him to North American waters so that at the start of the Seven Years War with France he had become Commander in Chief of the North American Squadron with successes in the Gulf of St Lawrence and in the capture of Quebec in 1759. Blockading duties off Brest in *Orford* and, later, *Mars* were so successful that in 1769 he was appointed Rear Admiral of the Blue. He attended the Naval Review at Spithead in 1773 and was later knighted by George III. Admiral Sir Richard Spry died and was buried at St Anthony in 1775 to be succeeded by his nephew, Thomas Davey, who adopted the name Spry. His career was less successful than that of his uncle but he too reached the rank of Admiral in 1805 when he retired to Place. Before he died in 1828 he added the lands of Killiganoon and Tregolls to the family estate. In 1851 Sir Thomas Spry restored the church at St Anthony, advised by the Revd Mr Carlyon, incumbent of the parish of St Just in Roseland, a keen wood-carver who restored many of the pew ends in both churches. The above view was created as recently as 1861, when Sir Samuel Spry altered the front of the house to resemble a French chateau and reclaimed the foreshore, where a tide mill is believed to have once worked, to create the lawns which set off the house so well, especially when the tide is high. North of the house, near the entrance to the creek, is Cellars Beach, named, it is thought, after pilchard cellars which stood here at one time, part of the very active fishing industry of St Mawes creek.

St Just creek is about a mile north of St Mawes. There is no village at St Just: the hamlet on the road above the creek is known as St Just Highway and has in the past served both fishing and farming communities. The creek offers a sheltered anchorage for small boats because of the shallow nature of its water at other than high tides. Boat building has been its most notable activity for over a century and the picture above shows Pascoe's boatyard in 1904 with two members of the family working on a large boat outside their shed. In the background, St Just bar appears to have grass on it – today it is covered with boats.

Of the seven waterside churches around the Fal estuary there can be little doubt that the most attractive setting is that of St Just church with its park-like burial ground. The isolation of the creek made it the ideal location for the harbour's quarantine station and a ship with any form of infectious disease on board would anchor there until cleared to enter Falmouth. In June 1820 the *Prince Ernest* packet, which had brought home the body of Lady Powerscourt, was being fumigated by four men using 'squibs' when, as reported in the *West Briton*, 'a spark accidentally' communicated itself with the magazine which had been incautiously left open'. The resulting explosion of 50 lb of gunpowder blew off the deck between the mainmast and the stern and caused the mainmast itself to shatter. Two men were badly injured and the damage cost over £700 to repair.

Once the Navy had belatedly acknowledged the advantages of steam-powered iron ships after 1850, many of the 'wooden walls' dating from the Nelson era were stationed in estuaries all round the British coast and used as training ships. In March 1866 HMS *Ganges* arrived in the harbour to be anchored in St Just Pool (left). Under the command of Capt. Frederick Hildebrand Stevens, the vessel arrived with 180 boys transferred from *Wellesley* at Chatham, but recruiting locally was slow to start with, allegedly on account of the harsh discipline and cruelty of the punishment on board. Capt. Stevens and his first lieutenant were replaced after only four months on station, after which numbers rose so that by August there were over 400 boys undergoing the rigorous training. Some boys came from poor families, while others were from workhouses. The picture below shows some of the boys with the crew of *Ganges* which consisted of both sailors and marines. The ship's police carried thick bamboo canes and the sailor-instructors a piece of knotted rope known as a 'stonnicky' and these were regularly used as part of the training methods then in fashion. Routine was arduous, starting at 5.30 a.m. with deck scrubbing in all weathers, and the boys went barefoot at all times, shoes worn only when going ashore. Instruction in rowing, sailing, gunnery (on obsolete weapons) and swimming was followed by 'recreation' with Indian clubs. Shore visits were restricted to rare games of football or marches around the lanes of the Mylor area. Sometimes concerts, theatrical performances or lantern lectures rounded off the day but the entire audience were likely to be sleeping soundly after the exertions of the day.

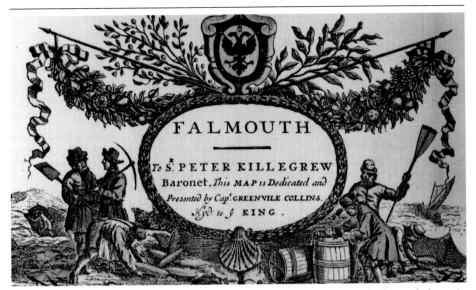

Lucas Waghenaer, a Dutchman, published the world's first volume of engraved charts in 1583. These were copied for Admiral Lord Howard of Effingham in 1588, just before the first Armada sailed, and from then onwards English sailors called any volume of charts 'Waggoners'. A century later, in the successive reigns of Charles II, James II and William of Orange, Captain Greenvile Collins was commissioned to chart the coasts of the whole of Great Britain and *Great Britain's Coasting Pilot* was published in 1693. Part of the chart of Falmouth harbour is reproduced below showing soundings, anchorages and rocks (marked as X). Each chart has an elaborate, decorative cartouche and that shown above bears a dedication to its sponsor, Sir Peter Killigrew.

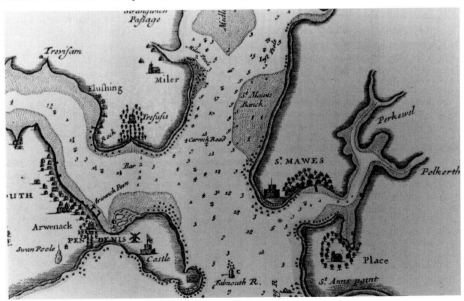

If only photography had been invented half a century earlier, our records of the Falmouth Packet Service would be so much more detailed and accurate. As it is, we must rely on descriptions, imaginative engravings and paintings, although an interesting record is the model shown above, now in Falmouth's Maritime Museum, of Capt. John Bull's packet *Duke of Marlborough*, made by the ship's carpenter for presentation to his captain. In front of the model stands Bull's famous silver pig which was stolen from his cabin but which was put up for auction some time later; he attended the sale, and when the article was produced his exclamation of 'Damn me! That's my pig!' dissuaded other bids and he regained possession quite cheaply. From its inception in 1688 the Packet Service had relied on privately owned vessels to carry the mails, but the Navy took over this duty in 1823. The naval brigs used for this were totally unsuited for sailing in the deep, exposed Atlantic waters, and of the first twelve in service seven were lost during the first year of operations with a total loss of life of 285 sailors. The picture below of *Nautilus*, one of the training brigs attached to *Ganges*, portrays the type of vessel probably used.

Pilots based in Falmouth and St Mawes were responsible not only for bringing large sailing vessels in and out of the harbour but also taking them up the English Channel or Irish Sea after receiving orders. *Warn's Directory* of 1864 records twenty-one pilots and eight cutters, apparently working independently until the Falmouth Pilot Boat Association was formed in 1887. By 1913 there were still twenty-one pilots, but only four cutters, one of which was *Arrow*, No. 6, seen above. She was built at Percuil, probably at the Peters' yard. The routine for these vessels consisted of a cruise at sea with five pilots aboard for three days on either the Lizard or Manacles station. Sometimes orders would be delivered to ships at sea, but most often inbound vessels would be boarded and taken into harbour. After three days at sea, the cutter would spend one day on harbour duty dealing with outward-bound craft, followed by another sea patrol. After its working life was over this stout vessel passed into private hands but was finally laid up in Froe creek where its skeletal remains are said to lie, still visible at low water (see *Falmouth* p. 122).

In June 1928 a large party of over 200 people set out to traverse the borough bounds, enlarged in 1892. Starting at Swanpool, they walked the land boundary which included the marshy land below Marlborough House for which purpose some, including the mayor and mayoress, had brought waders but many others, as the *Western Morning News* reported, 'had not done so and experienced quite a wetting'. In the afternoon a much reduced party of less than a hundred embarked in the steamer *St Mawes* to beat the water bounds and, as the section inside the harbour took longer than planned, it was decided to postpone the remainder until another day. It was not until September that the ritual was completed by a large party including girl guides, boy scouts and borough officials. As the steamer could not put the party ashore at Rosemullion, as many as possible went ashore in the rowing boat shown above.

Three windjammers and one steamer lying at anchor in lower Carrick Roads typify the use to which this large sheltered harbour has been put ever since man has used the sea as a means of transport. Early historians, with a degree of exaggeration, have said that a hundred vessels could lie here without seeing each others' tops'ls. In 1506, when a ship carrying the King and Queen of Castile home to Spain was stormbound in the harbour, the Venetian Ambassador to Castile wrote: 'We are in a very wild place which no human being ever visits, in the midst of a most barbarous race, so different in language and custom from the Londoners and the rest of England that they are as unintelligible to these last as to the Venetians.' More recent accounts such as that in Philp's *Panorama of Falmouth* (1827) recount how, in severe weather in 1815, eight ships of war with 300 vessels in convoy, together with another 100 coasters, rode out the storm for three weeks in perfect safety. Similarly, in November 1838, nearly 200 windbound vessels safely rode out several days of gale, and an unusual feature of this particular storm was that the strong winds, coinciding with a spring tide, caused the sea to rise so high that considerable damage was done to cellars and quays along the Falmouth waterfront. Sometimes, when strong winds blew from the south or south-east, some damage was done in the harbour when ships dragged their anchors. In one storm in 1867 the barque *Yorkshire* ran on to Bar beach half-full of water, the Portugese brig *Iberia* with a cargo of wine went ashore on Trefusis Point, the schooner *Vesta* drifted up the Penryn river and grounded after colliding with the Dutch barque *Luconia*, while nine other vessels cut away their masts and rigging to reduce the effect of the wind and nineteen others were sunk or damaged. As a result of so many ships losing their anchors there arose in the most favourable anchorages a considerable hazard on the harbour floor, and in October 1868 several lighters with sixty riggers came from Plymouth to raise the anchors and chains lying in the fairway off St Mawes Castle; a week or so later eleven anchors and 500 fathoms of chain went on sale on the quay. War in other countries was sometimes the reason for vessels remaining in Carrick Roads for long periods. In July 1848 forty ships of ten different flags were reported to be waiting at anchor on account of 'disturbances' in their countries, and the Agents G.C. Fox and Co. hired the tug *Sydney*, belonging to the Redruth and Chacewater Railway, to take the captains, their consuls and some of the town's merchants to Glendurgan Gardens for an excursion on the Helford River. There were times, however, when there were few ships at anchor, and in April 1890 the *West Briton* reported that the harbour 'presented a most unusual appearance: on the whole of the magnificent roadstead, extending from St Anthony's lighthouse to Mylor pool, not a single vessel, with the exception of HMS *Ganges*, was at anchor'. But, for many years, before radio became an essential part of a ship's equipment, a steady stream of large sailing vessels came to Falmouth 'for orders', when the owners would tell the captain where to take the vessel to unload. This became particularly important after it had been discovered in the mid-nineteenth century that iron ships would float and the size of sailing vessels increased greatly. The large three- and four-masted barquentines came to Europe from all over the world carrying huge cargoes of non-perishable commodities in their cavernous holds having left port with the instructions to go to 'Falmouth for Orders'. This gave rise to some of the famous 'grain races' from Australia, as in January 1929 when *Herzogin Cecile* (laden with 52,000 bags of wheat), *Beatrice* (36,000 bags) and *Lawhill* (56,000 bags) sailed from Port Lincoln in South Australia and on May 10 *Herzogin Cecile* arrived first after 104 days. Her fastest passage had been 88 days (see *Falmouth* p. 127).

Passat (above) is one of many magnificent windjammers to have visited Falmouth 'for orders' and, in so doing, brought considerable trade to the port. The robust sailing boats called 'quay punts' (see p. 94) would sail out past the Lizard to meet incoming vessels and arrange to act as one vessel's 'tender' as long as she remained in port. Today the only ships of this type likely to be seen in the port are those such as the Danish training ship *Christian Raddich* (below) taking part in the 1966 and 1982 Tall Ships Races, both of which started from Falmouth.

SALVAGED GOODS FOR SALE

To be Sold **By Auction at**

CADGWITH, LIZARD & FALMOUTH
Thursday, 10th October. 1872
and other various dates

The whole of the

Sails, Rigging, Spars, Windlasses, a Patent Double Purchase Capstan, Boats, Anchors, Cables, a Large Number of Lots of Timber, Planking, Hempen Wire, Copper and Yellow Metal Bolts, Sheathing, Iron and Other Materials salved from the two Italian Barques 'Marrianne' and 'Nuevo Raffaelino' upwards of 700 tons register. Both vessels were wrecked on The Lizard Rocks on 12th September last whilst on passage from Bassein. The above items will be found in first rate condition, the Ships being nearly new and their outfit in a very superior condition.

Also 400 Bags of damaged Rice will be offered for sale, and a large number of empty Rice Sacks. Bad weather makes it extremely doubtful whether any more of the Rice Cargos will be salvaged.

For further particulars apply to Messrs. G. C. Fox & Co., Falmouth or the Auctioneer, Henry Pollard

7th October, 1872

In May 1872 two Genoese barques left Bassein in Burma loaded with rice: *Marrianne*, 700 tons, and *Nuevo Raffaelino* met up three months later off the Isles of Scilly and sailed on together until separated by fog and on 21 September both went aground on the Stags, south of the Lizard, unaware of each other's fate until the crews met up on shore. The sea-swollen rice burst open the hulls and the result can be seen in the poster opposite. Such sales were commonplace in Cornwall: derelicts, or ships abandoned in storm by the crew but later found and towed in by another vessel, were often towed into Falmouth as the first port in the English Channel. Both vessels pictured on this page arrived in this way. In November 1880 the 795-ton iron barque *Gileena*, having lost two masts and been abandoned, was brought in by the German mail steamer *Leipzig* after a tow of 400 miles lasting four days. The 'prize' carried a cargo of maize and baled cotton which, with the ship, was later sold locally. Local newspapers frequently advertised such sales and the poster opposite is typical of the many with which the town's notice boards were covered.

MR. CORFIELD

WILL SELL BY

PUBLIC AUCTION

In Convenient Lots, at and near the
Stores of Messrs. W. & E.C. Carne,

MARKET STREET, FALMOUTH,

On FRIDAY next, 28th March,

At 3 o'clock in the Afternoon,

THE FOLLOWING

Wool and Effects,

(Salved from the above Wreck,) comprising

Several HIDES, AWNINGS, SAILS, and
PIECES of DITTO, MANILLA WARP,
CORDAGE, JUNK, MATS, and
numerous other Articles.

TOGETHER WITH

From 2000 to 3000 lbs.

OF BUENOS AYRIAN WOOL,

4 to 5 Tons Brass, Copper, Lead, and Old Metal.

*To View and for further Particulars apply at
the Offices of the said*

Messrs. W. & E. C. Carne,

or the   Agents for the River Parana
Steam Ship Company, Limited,

Auctioneer, Falmouth.

Dated March 20th, 1873,

Preliminary Notice.

FOR THE BENEFIT OF THE CONCERNED.
Wreck of the S. S. Clan Alpine.

MR. CORFIELD

Will submit to Public Auction, on or about
the first week in November, at the Docks,
Falmouth, an immense quantity of

Wrought Plate and Cast

IRON

many hundreds of Condensing Brass Tubes,
with various other portions of the Machin-
ery, Heavy Chain Cables, old Metal, in
Brass, Copper, and Lead, and numerous
Effects. See subsequent advertisements.
Dated Auction Offices, October 15th, 1873.

In an easterly blizzard on 2 February 1873, the
Clan Alpine, a 1,500-ton brigantine-rigged
steamer launched in Glasgow eleven years earlier and belonging to the River Parana Steamship
Company, struck the menacing rocks off Black
Head two miles south of the Manacles. Eighteen
were saved, including one passenger, but the
captain and twelve others were lost and buried
together in St Keverne churchyard. The valuable
cargo comprised timber, silver ore, copper
ingots, hides, rape seed and foodstuffs, and
extensive salvage operations took place over the
next few months organized by W. and E.C.
Carne, the owner's agents in Falmouth. The
variety of material salvaged is shown in this
extract from the *Commercial, Shipping and
General Advertiser for West Cornwall* (better
known as the *Penryn Advertiser*). The first sale
(top), dated 20 March 1873, took place at
Carne's stores in Market Street and consisted
largely of cargo and sails; the second (below),
some seven months later, included parts of the
vessel and its engines and took place at the
Docks. From such sales local traders, shipbuilders and boat owners obtained much valuable material comparatively cheaply.

(Opposite.) In times of war, when Royal Navy
vessels captured enemy ships as 'prizes', their
cargoes were sold by auction and the prize
money divided among the ships making the capture. This was a considerable incentive to
recruitment as the Crown waived its right to
such prize money after 1692, and the Cruisers
Act of 1708 allocated the whole of the value to
the captors, dividing it into eighths, of which
the captain had three parts, commander-in-
chief, officers and warrant officers one each,
and the crew two. Not surprisingly some naval
officers became very rich in this way. Sometimes
the captured ships were put into service by the
captors without changing the name, and in the
Battle of Trafalgar the French had *Swiftsure* and
Berwick while the original *Temeraire* was captured by Admiral Boscawen at Lagos in 1759.

CAPTURED FROM THE

FRENCH

by Squadrons of His Majesties Frigates this valuable

PRIZE

WHICH WILL BE EXPOSED FOR SALE AT

WYNNS HOTEL, FALMOUTH

Tuesday the 13th day of March, 1798

AT 10 O'CLOCK IN THE FORENOON, CONSISTING OF A CHOICE ASSORTMENT OF

Wheat Flour, 75 bags and 7 casks
Wine of good quality, 684 Hogs Heads and 28 Casks
Oak Timber, large, for shipbuilding
Rosin, 1228 cakes
Casks (empty) and a parcel
Soap, 20 chests
Cordials, 4 baskets
Salt (French), 11451 bushels
Callavancies, beans and pease
Hats, 2 casks
Deals, 200 pieces

Beef and Salt Pork, 123 barrels
Starch, 12 barrels
Ships Bread, 463 casks
Dunnage Plank, 1 cwt. 3 qtrs. 12 lb.
Wood Hoops, 148 bundles
Tobacco, 17 bales and a hogshead
Boots, a basket
Geneva, 8 casks
Turpentine, 24 casks
Brandy, 24 pieces and 3 heads
A parcel of staves and hoops
Beer, 28 hogsheads

A very large Crane, all complete, capable of raising the greatest weights, also one large ships anchor of about 3 tons and several small anchors.
Sundry items of gunners stores.

Being the entire cargoes of the French Ships Le Benjamin. A Chasse Maree. La Thane. La Nancy. Le St. Roissoeurs. Le Furet. Le Dauphin. Le St. Jean Baptiste. La St. Anne. Le St. Peter and La St. Rene. Also stores from the privateers La Rayon. Le Zephir. L'Hyanee. Le Vengeur and L'Henreuse, all lately taken on the French coast and off Spain by ships of His Majesty King George III.

GOD SAVE THE KING

HENRY WILLIAMS. Falmouth.
3rd February. 1798

On 15 July 1899 the largest vessel to have entered Falmouth harbour did so in the unfortunate circumstances shown in these four pictures. Six weeks before the crew of pilot cutter 13, on station near the Manacles soon after midnight on 21 May, were astonished to see the American liner *Paris*, with 370 crew and 380 passengers, 'pass like a train at 18 knots' and disappear into the foggy night bound for the disaster shown on this page. The cutter followed and found the liner firmly grounded on rocks a few hundred yards off Lowland Point, the largest vessel ever to have been stranded on the Cornish coast at that time. Exactly how lucky they had been became clear to passengers and crew when, at daybreak, they saw less than a mile to the north the masts of the *Mohegan* which had gone down less than a year before with the loss of 106 lives. The Falmouth tug *Triton* towed out Falmouth lifeboat, and assisted by the Porthoustock lifeboat safely transferred all passengers to hotels in Falmouth. The London Salvage Association took charge of the six-week rescue operation. German and Swedish salvage vessels were aided by the Falmouth tug *Dragon* in the patching and pumping work until, on the night of 14 July, on a

southerly wind and high tide, *Paris* rose to clear the rocks and the pumps were able to keep the vessel afloat. The fleet arrived off St Anthony lighthouse soon after midnight but had to anchor because of low tide. Next morning the Falmouth harbourmaster was surprised to see this flotilla slowly entering the harbour. *Paris* was edged into the Docks tidal basin with only one minor mishap when, as the local newspaper reported 'the vessel fell foul of the eastern breakwater causing spectators to make off hurriedly'. The salvage vessels in the picture below are, left to right, local tug *Victor, Seeadler, Svitzer* (alongside, port side), *Berthilde* (barely visible) and extreme right, local tug *Dragon*. None of the dry docks was big enough to take *Paris* for repair, but in the four weeks she was in Falmouth she proved a boon to local traders as thousands of visitors came by train to see this unusual sight. Eventually, on 15 August, *Paris* was towed to Milford Haven for repair. Renamed *Philadelphia* she ran on to the rocks of Rame Head near Plymouth on 14 January 1914 but was towed off with a dented hull.

CAPTURED GERMAN LINER 'PRINZ ADALBERT' AT FALMOUTH AUG 1914

Following the outbreak of the First World War in August 1914, many German vessels, such as the *Kron Prinz Adalbert* shown above, were captured at sea by the Royal Navy and brought into Falmouth (see *Falmouth* p. 136). Several more captured German ships are shown below moored close to the American cruisers *Tennessee* and *North Carolina*, which had nothing to do with their capture as the USA did not declare war until 1917. Falmouth had an indirect connection with the American entry into the war. When their submarine offensive began in 1915 the Germans pledged not to sink American ships, but withdrew the pledge in 1917 and tried to impose restrictions on American shipping contacts with Britain. One of these was that only one US passenger vessel per week would be allowed to visit this country at Falmouth on condition that it was painted with alternate red and white vertical stripes three yards wide and flew a red and white chequered flag on each mast. Not surprisingly, the Americans refused to observe such conditions and the worsened relations led eventually to a declaration of war.

Steam tug *Triton*, 10 tons, belonging to the Falmouth Towage Company, is seen here 'coaling' alongside one of the coal hulks in the harbour. In the early days of steam this operation was carried out entirely by man-power, and the coal was sold by Gueret, Llewellyn and Merrett (often called GLM), who described themselves as 'colliery agents', from their base in the building on North Quay. Another hulk was moored alongside the Northern Arm in the Docks, but as ships grew larger and demand increased in the 1920s and early 1930s the business became mechanized and two coal 'elevators' *Penair* and *Mariman* were stationed in the harbour to refuel vessels more quickly.

The steamship *Duchess of Cornwall* of the Chellew Line left Swansea on Christmas morning in 1912 with a cargo of coal for Leghorn under command of Captain Yeo of Tywardreath. Meeting with a severe gale off Lands End, the captain made for Falmouth, but off the Lizard the vessel was hit by a huge wave which tore away the lifeboats and funnel in addition to the hand steering gear and all deck fittings. The first mate and a sailor were lost overboard and water poured in so that the captain in the chart room was up to his neck in water. The ship's disaster signals were not seen and the crew fought for hours to bring her into Falmouth where she is seen above, anchored in Carrick Roads with four feet of water in the cabins and a heavy list to port.

Launched on 20 September 1910, HMS *Falmouth* was a second class protected cruiser built by Beardmore and Company at Dalmuir, Scotland. With a displacement of 5,250 tons, her length was 450 ft, beam 49 ft and she cost £339,000. She was commissioned on 1 September 1911 and visited Falmouth for five days a month later, when the officers and crew were entertained in the town and the ship was opened to visitors. Captain Grant and his officers were entertained by the mayor and Corporation at a banquet at the Royal Hotel on 2 November when a beautiful rose bowl (inset) was presented to the ship by the mayor, Alderman F.J. Bowles, on behalf of the townspeople. Later the mayor and Corporation were entertained on the ship (below) and, sitting in the front row, left to right are: First Lieutenant May, Alderman J. Grose, Captain Grant, Alderman F.J. Bowles, Alderman Bullen, Alderman Williams and the ship's chaplain, Lieutenant Lloyd.

These three German submarines or U-boats, seen here lying alongside the Northern Arm, were part of a group of eight vessels brought to Falmouth in 1921 for testing and experimental purposes. The remains of four lie on the floor of Falmouth Bay; the others were abandoned on the rocks on the west side of Pendennis Point where they lay as a playground for local children until the Second World War when they were almost entirely destroyed as part of the drive for scrap metal (see *Falmouth* p. 140). Accompanying the submarines was the grotesque salvage vessel *Cyklops* consisting of two identical hulls firmly attached to each other by a sturdy gantry surmounted by the bridge. Seen here moored to a buoy in the harbour, the function of this craft was to lift the submarines into the space between the hulls for repair and maintenance.

On board this motor yacht *Harbinger* in Falmouth harbour in January 1912 'Monte Carlo Wells', who twenty years earlier had 'broken the bank' in the Casino there and so inspired the famous music-hall song, was arrested. Wells, who was accompanied by a French woman, was found to have thirty-six aliases when arrested in connection with a fraud in France involving three million francs. The arrest was carried out by a French detective and PC Herbert Crocker, a French-speaking member of the Cornwall County Constabulary who retired in 1931 as an Inspector after thirty-two years' service.

On 14 August 1902 this small motor launch dropped anchor in Falmouth harbour after a 37-day voyage from New York, a rare occurrence in those days for such a small vessel. Capt. William C. Newman and his sixteen-year-old son Edward had been engaged by the New York Kerosene Company to test the reliability of a new engine, and during the voyage had experienced storms, leaking fuel pipes, shortage of fresh food and several near-misses with larger vessels. The *Abiel Abbot Low* was beached on the Bar to remove a thick layer of barnacles and before its departure for London, Mr J.C. Badger, Chaplain of the Seamen's Bethel, conducted a thanksgiving service at which 'the crowded sailor congregation gave the plucky voyagers a hearty reception' and each was presented with a silver cigarette case.

These J-Class yachts are racing in the Bay in 1934 with the distinctive Falmouth Hotel in the background. This class evolved as a result of British participation – and, usually, failure – in races for the America's Cup. The New York Yacht Club allotted letters to different classes, 'J' indicating 76 ft to 87 ft on the waterline. All British owners were very rich men such as Sir Thomas Lipton (*Shamrock*, right), W.F.S. Stephenson (*Velsheda*, centre) and Hugh F. Paul (*Astra*, left); others were rich Americans, but they rarely appeared in British waters. Wherever they sailed these magnificent vessels employed professional crews, many of them local boatmen, who were glad of regular employment during the summer months. Their visits to Falmouth involved two days racing each year and were part of the regattas of the Royal Cornwall Yacht Club and the Port of Falmouth between 1926 and 1936 (except for 1932). During these ten years thirteen J-Class yachts came to Falmouth although no more than six raced in any one year. In addition to those in the photograph, they were *Britannia* (King George V), *White Heather* (Lord Waring), *Westward* (T.F.B. Davis), *Lulworth* (Sir Mortimer Singer), *Cambria* (Lord Camrose), *Candida* (H.A. Andreae), *Shamrock V* (C.R. Fairey), *Endeavour I and II* (T.O.M. Sopwith) and *Yankee* (Gerard P. Lambert, the only American). The most frequent visitor was *Britannia* which came here eight times, but after King George died in 1936 the yacht was towed out into the Channel and sunk; her flag was acquired by the RCYC, framed and hung in the smoking room. Such enormous vessels had disadvantages, one of which was the regularity with which they were dismasted in strong winds. Their end was brought about in the late 1930s by a number of factors: the death of the King ending the opportunity for rich owners to socialize in royal circles, the realization that smaller yachts were not only cheaper but were able to survive strong winds, and, finally, the outbreak of the Second World War which resulted in all American J-Class yachts being scrapped as part of the war effort. Short-lived though they were, they must have been a superb sight as they raced around Falmouth Bay.

Falmouth's most distinguished nautical resident was undoubtedly *Cutty Sark* which was anchored off Trefusis Point (below) between 1923 and 1938 as a boys' training ship. Brought to the port and restored to her former glory by Captain Dowman, her figure-head (above) shows 'Nannie', the beautiful witch who wore the 'cutty sark' or short shirt after which the vessel is named. Her left hand (obscured in this picture) has its fingers clenched, reaching for the mare's tail ridden by the legendary Tam o' Shanter in Robert Burns' poem. It is said that after a fast passage home the ships' apprentices would tease out a rope's end to represent the tail and put it into the outstretched hand (see *Falmouth* p. 126). Below, *Cutty Sark* is seen with *Foudroyant*, anchored together off Trefusis Point (details of *Foudroyant* are given on p. 43).

Falmouth has been used in wartime as an emergency base for seaplanes but this has never been a recognized part of the harbour's activities. The somewhat incongruous picture above, showing extreme examples of naval warfare, was taken in the 1920s when experiments were taking place to assess the harbour's suitability for such aircraft and they were moored to buoys in the inner harbour not far from *Foudroyant* (right) and *Cutty Sark*. Further trials in the 1930s, using Short Singapore, Mark 3 aircraft (below) led to nothing, although there was an equally short-lived plan after the Second World War to use the harbour as a base for Sunderland aircraft to carry passengers to the Isles of Scilly. *Foudroyant* was a training ship brought to the port by Mr Wheatley Cobb in 1905. After the original *Foudroyant* had been destroyed by fire off Blackpool in June 1897, he bought and renamed *Trincomalee*, a 38-gun frigate built in Bombay in 1817. She was a familiar part of the Falmouth harbour scene, fondly remembered by many long-term residents, until her departure to Portsmouth in 1929.

Another Wheatley Cobb acquisition was *Implacable*, seen here arriving in the port in 1912. This philanthropist maintained both vessels in Falmouth for use by boys training for a life at sea, but during the depression of the late 1920s he found it increasingly difficult to maintain the ships. In a letter which he wrote to the *Falmouth Packet* in September 1929, he said: '. . . £30,000 has been spent on her . . . she is now a thoroughly sound ship with accommodation for 250 boys. So far her occupants have been Navy League Cadets who come down for a fortnight. . . .' He went on to add, as part of his appeal for financial assistance, '. . . the collapse of the South Wales coal trade has reduced my income by half. . . .' but his appeal met with no success and *Implacable* was towed to Portsmouth in 1932 (see *Falmouth* p. 125).

Other 'wooden walls' stationed in the harbour at various times included HMS *Cambridge*, seen here at anchor with the unusual and unsightly addition on her deck of what appears to be a large shed, probably for living and training accommodation. Other similar vessels to have adorned the waters of Carrick Roads were *St George*, a guardship used by the Coastguard for gunnery training and removed, with much local protest, in 1865, and *Russell*, used for the same purpose. The *West Briton* reported in June 1859 that 250 Naval Coast Volunteers arrived in Truro by train, were marched to Malpas and embarked on the tender *Hind* to be taken downriver to *Russell*.

Falmouth has only been used as a naval base in times of national emergency. During the French Wars, from 1794 onwards, two squadrons of frigates were based here on patrol and blockade duties off the French coast and convoys assembled here under naval protection. In both world wars the harbour became a valuable strategic base, especially in preparation for the 1944 invasion of France (see p. 76). But most visits by naval craft have been for social reasons and the authorities have been keen to foster this to boost the town's trade. In August 1866 the *West Briton* reported the arrival in the bay of the Channel Squadron made up of six large ships, while frequent visitors were the torpedo boat fleet, shown above, described as 'the sooty and surreptitious imps of the main' in August 1887 when they announced their departure by 'arousing all inhabitants at four a.m. by their unearthly whistles. It is impossible to conceive without hearing them, the hideous sounds which can be emitted from steam whistles. Each boat has a distinguishing whistle and is known by its yell.' Larger vessels sometimes arrived, as shown below in July 1930, in Regatta week, when nine battleships accompanied by destroyers assembled and 3,000 sailors came ashore daily and clubs, churches and chapels were thrown open. The mayor, Mr George Butler, went out to HMS *Nelson* to extend a formal welcome to the fleet.

Tariff of Charges for Towing Fishing Boats.

Agreed on at a meeting of Tug Owners in the Chamber of Commerce, February 27th, 1897.

	Distance in miles.	When one boat only.	If 2 boats each to pay	If 3 boats each to pay	If 4 boats or more.
Castle & Shag Rock to Docks	—	5/-	3/9	3/4	A
Helford to Docks	—	10/-	7/6	6/8	further
Manacles ,,	6	20/-	17/-	13/4	Reduction
Blackhead ,,	11	30/-	22/6	20/-	by
Lizard ,,	17	40/-	30/-	26/8	agreement.
Wolf ,,	40	120/-	90/-	80/-	

Intermediate distances between Lizard and Wolf, and beyond the Wolf, to be arranged at a charge proportionate to the Lizard Rate.

Outwards.—Each boat to pay half the Inward Rate for single boat, irrespective of number towed.

Steam Tugs Belonging to the Port.

Name.	Tons.	H.P.	Owners.
DRAGON..	6	90	Falmouth Towage Co.
EAGLE	13	80	Eagle Trawling & Towage Company.
MARION..	2	24	Marion S.S. Co., Ltd.
*NEW RESOLUTE ..	14	25	River Fal S.S. Co.
BRITON	1.5	24	W. Rowe.
TRITON	10	99	Falmouth Towage Co.
VICTOR	17	95	Thomas and Hancock.
*PRINCESS VICTORIA	28	26	River Fal S.S. Co.
*QUEEN OF THE FAL	31	28	River Fal S.S. Co.

Steamers "Alexandra" and "Roseland" trading between Falmouth and St. Mawes (passenger boats), and the boarding boats "Perran" (Fox & Co.), "Lizard" (Broad & Sons), "Norman" (Cox & Co.), "Carbon" (Falmouth Coal Co.), "Arwenack" (Falmouth Harbour Board), "Fawn" (P. Carlyle), and "Leander" (Flushing Ferry Boat), are not included in the above list.

* Registered at Truro.

Falmouth owes an enormous debt of gratitude to the Lake family who, for many years up to 1939, regularly published directories and almanacs. The page-advert reproduced here is taken from their 1913 *Almanac* and gives a fascinating insight into a use of tugs which is not commonly known yet must have been a regular feature of their work: towing fishing boats – often several at a time – to and from the Docks which was then the base for fish landing operations (see p. 62).

The smallest of all the harbour tugs, *Marion*, steaming back into the harbour, belonged to the Marion Steamship Company, directors of which were A.W. Chard, W.J. Thomas, H. Newton, H.J.R. Corlyon, T.A. Webber and John Chard. In 1914 the vessel was involved in an unusual incident when French aviator Henri Salmet was taking the mayoress, Mrs A.W. Chard on a pleasure flight to Penzance but engine trouble forced the sea-plane down off the Manacles: the coastguard called out *Marion* which towed the plane to Penzance with the mayoress on board.

William Rowe, owner of Kergilliack Farm and proprietor of two butchers shops in the town, became involved in shipping in the 1890s with a 90 ft tug *Penguin* (see p. 49) built by Cox and Co. who also built a second larger tug of the same name which is illustrated here. Both vessels were sea-going tugs operating to ports on both sides of the English Channel although they carried passengers in the holiday season on excursions along the coast. Much more information on these interesting craft is given in *Passenger Steamers of the River Fal* by Alan Kittridge.

This must have been a familiar sight in Falmouth Bay up to the early 1930s: the windjammer *Malgwyn* approaches the harbour entrance in calm weather, anchors 'at cock bill', ready to let go, and escorted by two steam vessels which are probably the pilot boat *Pendragon* (left) and tug *New Resolute*. In the heyday of 'Falmouth for Orders' it was not unusual for over a hundred such sailing boats to be coming and going in the approaches to Falmouth, resulting in steady work for the port's boats as well as the town's traders.

The ten-ton tug *Triton* belonging to the Falmouth Towage Company must have been involved in many such arrivals as well as departures when the sailing vessels were towed out into the open sea to catch the wind. The Falmouth Towage Company, with offices at 17 Arwenack Street, was established in 1882 and is still in business today, based in the Docks.

Apart from their very early days, paddle steamers have never been common in Falmouth harbour and, here, *Princess Royal* has come from her home river, the Tamar, probably on the day of Falmouth Regatta when she would take locals to view the day's racing in the harbour and bay. The limitations of the Market Strand Pier are seen clearly here and it was not long after this that the extension was added to create the Prince of Wales' Pier. On the near side is the Flushing ferry *Greyhound*, a wooden steamer which came to the harbour from Plymouth in 1888 when she was fitted with an engine at Sara's Penryn foundry. The Falmouth end of the Flushing ferry had moved to the Market Strand, where it remains today, just before *Greyhound's* arrival.

This photograph of about 1900 shows the congestion which took place in the summer months alongside the Market Strand Pier. Five steamers are seen here: from the right, they are *Roseland*, built by Cox and Co. for the St Mawes Steamship Company in 1886, Rowe's first *Penguin*, *Emperor* acquired by the River Fal Steamship Company in 1882, with the distinctive cross on the funnel, the same company's *Victoria*, built by Cox and Co. in 1900, and the stern of an unidentified passenger vessel on the extreme left.

Up to the early years of the twentieth century several small, family-run companies controlled the passenger traffic in the estuary, but in 1906 the organizations of W.J. Thomas and family, A.W. Chard and the Benny Company amalgamated to form the River Fal Steamship Company. The fleet consisted of *Queen of the Fal*, built by Cox and Co. in 1893, and *New Resolute*, a wooden vessel from the Malpas yard of Scoble and Davies. Soon after the amalgamation *Princess Victoria* (seen below) was built in the Cox yard. *Queen of the Fal* was sold in 1911 but a new vessel with the same name was added in 1912 and this was used for coastal trips while *Princess Victoria* was used in the estuary and river. She is seen here alongside the new Prince of Wales' Pier, now extended to over 100 yd in length on what, from the number of passengers and their dress, seems to be a somewhat inclement day. After service in the First World War the boats returned to excursion and ferry duties but economies forced the sale of *New Resolute* in 1926 when the price of coal had risen alarmingly and few

THE RIVER FAL STEAMSHIP CO.,

* * LIMITED, * *

Will run their favourite and well-appointed Steamers

"Princess Victoria"

"Queen of the Fal"

and "New Resolute"

Daily during the summer months and twice weekly during the winter months from **Falmouth** up the Beautiful River Fal to **Truro**.

**Return Fare, 1/3; Children under twelve. 9d.
Single, 1/-; Children, 6d.**

Return Fare between Malpas and Falmouth (without landing), 1/-; Children, 6d.

Charming Harbour and Coast Trips

During the summer season, full particulars of which are advertised weekly in local papers.

Great Western Railway Circular Trip Tickets are taken and issued on board these Steamers.

For times of starting see Bills and Local Newspapers, or apply to the Managers:—CAPTAIN A. BENNEY, Falmouth; Mr. W. J. THOMAS, Falmouth; Mr. H. J. R. CORLYON, *Secretary*, Falmouth, or to the Captains on Board.

people could afford holidays during the depression. During the Second World War both remaining vessels left the port on war service and the company was wound up.

In 1900 Messrs Thomas and Chard had *Victoria* built by Cox and Co: this 67-ton 82 ft vessel was used between Falmouth and Truro (or Malpas at low tide), but after only one year of work she was sold and another *Victoria* was built in the Cox yard. Here, the first of that name lies off Flushing while awaiting the arrival of the occupants of the rowing boat.

In 1938 the St Mawes Steam Tug and Passenger Company bought a three-year-old steel motor vessel from a Yorkshire company and renamed her *New Roseland*, seen here against St Mawes quay. During the war the vessel was taken to the Bristol Channel and used as a support vessel for the balloon barrage in the area. Returned to her owners after the war, *New Roseland* became part of a fleet of four passenger vessels which the company operated on ferry and excusion services in and outside the estuary until declining business resulted in two vessels being sold in 1968, and two years later *New Roseland* joined them on the Thames. Only one launch now remained to operate the St Mawes ferry and the company was wound up.

Several of Falmouth's passenger-tugs remained in the port for a long time: *Victor* was one of these. Having been built in the yard of Pool, Skinner and Williams on the Bar and fitted with Cox engines in 1898, she survived until 1934 when, as the last independent passenger-tug in the port, she was sold to a South Wales owner. In those thirty-six years she had been easily recognizable by the Maltese cross on her funnel, a feature inherited from her predecessor, *Emperor*. Some of her earliest work was involved with the wrecks of *Mohegan* and *Paris* on the Manacles, in the latter case ferrying the passengers to Falmouth and, afterwards, running excursions to the salvage site. In the picture above she is seen going astern away from Prince of Wales' Pier before setting out on an excursion; below, she is steaming at speed towards the harbour entrance on one of the coastal excursions for which she was noted, visiting any point between the Lizard and Plymouth.

Between the wars towage became increasingly the monopoly of the Falmouth Towage Company and its tugs with their distinctive black and white funnels became part of the Falmouth harbour scene. Here, anchored off the town's waterfront are, left to right: *Lynch*, *St Merryn*, *Codicote Scot* (later *St Levan*), *Northgate Scot* (later *St Denys*), *Norgrove* (later *St Eval*) and *Fairnilee* (later *St Agnes*). All except *Lynch* were renamed after Cornish saints when P & O took over the Docks in 1974. The large vessel behind the tugs is the oil barge *Witonia*, while on the extreme right the funnel belongs to the floating crane *Titania*, more details of which appear on p. 74. Of the tugs in the picture, only *St Denys* has survived: after a few years moored in the Town Quay basin in Falmouth as part of the Maritime Museum, financial stringency forced her sale to a similar institution in Douarnenez in Brittany; all the others have been broken up.

Over the Christmas period of 1951 gales were raging in mid-Atlantic and ships were taking the usual precautions in such circumstances. One of these was the American freighter *Flying Enterprise*, 6,711 tons, with a general cargo bound for Hamburg. She hove to as winds reached hurricane force 450 miles west of Lands End but one enormous wave hit the ship with tremendous force and left her with the hull severely split and a 50 degree list to port. As the vessel drifted south-eastwards, thirty-five passengers and crew were taken off by the US Transport *General Greely* and US destroyer *Southland* but Captain Kurt Carlsen declined to leave his ship while she still floated – this act turned what might have been simply another shipping casualty into headline news around the world. For six days *Flying Enterprise* drifted with *General Greely* standing by until relieved by another US vessel *Golden Eagle*. Captain Dan Parker of the ocean salvage tug *Turmoil* (above) was anchored off Flushing when he received orders to sail immediately to assist the helplessly drifting freighter. Out in the Atlantic, US destroyer *John W. Weeks* had relieved other ships on the scene and managed to pass hot food to Captain Carlsen and *Turmoil* arrived on 3 January as the weather began to moderate by Atlantic standards. On 4 January, as

Turmoil passed within feet of the casualty, the mate Ken Dancey stepped from one ship to the other and in so doing passed into maritime legend with what the newspapers sensationalized as 'Dancey's Leap'. Every national newspaper had its representative at Falmouth where the apparatus room at the telephone exchange became a temporary news room, as seen here. Each reporter had a phone connection and apparatus to send pictures by wire. In the centre a smiling Mr Baden Rollason, engineer in charge, explains the workings to a reporter, watched by Arthur Brown, technical officer; in the background are Peter Strongman, engineer, and next to him is head postmaster Mr Percy Evans. Out in the Atlantic, the two protagonists finally succeeded in establishing a tow at 9.30 a.m. on 5 January with *Flying Enterprise* now listing at 70 degrees, down by the head with the split in her hull widening. The tow continued slowly through 6 and 7 January at 3 knots towards the north-east but chafing of the tow line was becoming a problem, to try and remedy which a can of butter was passed across to Ken Dancey. With deteriorating weather and heavy seas sweeping the *Flying Enterprise*, the tow parted after 250 miles as a result of heavy chafing soon after midnight on 9 January. *Flying Enterprise* was drifting 21 miles south of the Lizard and, after sixteen days, the drama was entering its final stages. A log of that day, 10 January 1952, would read: 0800 wind close to gale force, *FE* listing at nearly 90 degrees. 1400 *FE* losing buoyancy, lying lower in the water. 1430 port wing of the bridge under water. 1445 vessel foundering; Carlsen and Dancey ready to abandon ship. 1522 Carlsen and Dancey walk along the funnel and jump into the sea. 1531 recovered from the water and taken to sick bay. 1540 *Turmoil* heads for Falmouth with survivors on board. 1611 *FE* sank 43 miles south-east of Falmouth. When *Turmoil* reached Falmouth, Carlsen and Dancey were accorded a hero's welcome by the town and the civic reception by the mayor, Mr T.L. Morris appeared on the front pages of newspapers all over the world.

On 29 May 1959 the 9,200 ton Greek-owned, Liberian-registered *Mitera Marigo*, with a cargo of iron ore, collided with the German steamer *Fritz Rhysen* in dense fog off Ushant, the French equivalent of Lands End. Falmouth's tugs were summoned to tow her in and, later the same day, she entered Carrick Roads as seen above. As she was likely to founder, the vessel was towed towards a shallow part of the harbour but sank on the edge of the deep channel, directly opposite where the *Stanwood* had sunk twenty years before. Only the masts remained above the water, as shown below. Because of the danger of oil pollution from her fuel tanks the wreck was surrounded by a boom which was only partly successful but the local oyster beds seemed not to suffer any damage. Most of the cargo was salvaged and the wreck partially destroyed with explosives over the next two years so as not to be a hazard to navigation; now lying in about 80 ft of water, the wreck is marked on Admiralty charts of the harbour.

On 14 June 1968 a small ketch sailed almost unnoticed out of Falmouth harbour, on board a 30-year-old ex-Merchant Navy officer aiming to be the first to sail single-handed, non-stop round the world. On 22 April 1969, 312 days later, Robin Knox Johnston sailed back past Black Rock and into the pages of history, accompanied by a fleet of small boats. His return, with its media coverage, crowds of cheering spectators and civic reception, was in complete contrast with his departure ten and a half months earlier. In *A World of my Own* written later in 1969 Robin Knox Johnston gives a wonderful description of the dangers, problems, accidents and pleasures encountered by *Suhaili* on her circumnavigation. On his arrival in Falmouth, Harry Morgan, officer of the Customs and Excise was the first to board *Suhaili* and asked 'Where from?' to which the reply was 'Falmouth'. Since Dwight Long sailed across the Atlantic in his yacht *Idle Hour* in the late 1930s such crossings have become almost commonplace, with boats of ever-decreasing size and shape. Experienced sailors are able to cope with most problems likely to be encountered on such journeys, but when people with no knowledge of the sea arrive with the intention of sailing away in a bath or oil-drum, the rescue authorities become justifiably apprehensive.

This interesting view shows how the harbour looked after a spell of bad weather when many vessels had found refuge in its sheltered waters. Larger craft would anchor in the outer harbour or Carrick Roads while the smaller coastal schooners and ketches, seen above, came further in to assemble in the inner harbour or Penryn river. All except the rather incongruous white-hulled steam yacht in the foreground are small sailing boats, probably drying their sails in preparation for their departure. The slopes of Trefusis Point and the hills north of St Mawes are covered with snow which suggests that this picture may have been taken soon after the Great Blizzard of March 1891 when hurricane force winds accompanied by heavy snow caused enormous damage on land and sea. Railway lines blocked by deep drifts, fallen trees and telegraph poles meant that passengers were stranded for up to thirty-six hours in places, but it was at sea that damage and disaster was at its worst. Lifeboats could not be launched, breeches-buoy rockets could not be fired, and lives were lost in full view of the land as many vessels were driven ashore; fishing boats at anchor broke loose and were destroyed on rocks, while some of those at sea disappeared without trace. Falmouth Bay and harbour felt the full force of the south-easterly gale and on Nare Head, south of the Helford River entrance, the *Bay of Panama*, en route from Calcutta to Dundee with 17,000 bales of jute, was wrecked and eighteen of those of board, including the captain's wife, either drowned or froze to death in the rigging where they climbed to avoid the waves sweeping over the wreck of the four-masted barquentine. Survivors were rescued after twelve hours by the coastguard breeches-buoy apparatus when the wind was less violent, and taken to St Keverne farm. Taken by bus to Gweek later, they had to walk to Falmouth through deep snow and were finally looked after at the Royal Cornwall Sailors' Home. There were ten other known wrecks in the Falmouth area, and survivors were cared for either at the Sailors' Home or by the Shipwrecked Mariners' Aid Society, both of which fed and clothed their charges before supplying them with a free railway ticket to their home and food for the journey. For weeks afterwards the coastline was strewn with wreckage and many unidentified bodies were washed ashore.

SECTION TWO
The Waterfront

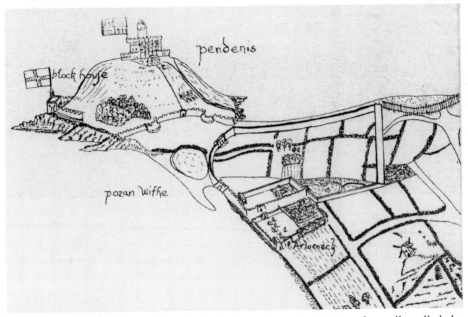

This extract from a map of the whole harbour drawn in 1580 and usually called the Burghley Map shows the stretch of shoreline that is now Falmouth's waterfront. Towns first grew up at the head of the creeks in the estuary – Truro, Tregony and Penryn – because the shores near the open sea were open to attack from hostile countries or from pirates. Penzance was sacked by the Spanish in 1589 and St Mawes was the object of more than one Breton attack in the fourteenth and sixteenth centuries. Even after Henry VIII had built the castles at the harbour entrance, the Killigrews, behind the walls of the fortified Arwenack House, were not eager to develop their estate until a visit by Sir Walter Raleigh in 1596 suggested it. The Pendennis fortifications shown here illustrate two interesting features of the peninsula's history: the 'blockhouse' shown at the water's edge was at one time much more extensive than today's Little Dennis fort, and the Castle itself, on the flat top of the promontory, consists solely of the keep of the present structure. Only in 1599 were the walled moat and enceinte built and, later, when an attack from the landward side was thought likely, the Hornworks were built north of the Castle as additional defences.

This may be one of the earliest photographs ever taken of Falmouth Docks. Not only is there a preponderance of sailing vessels in the inner harbour and two windjammers in the tidal basin but the *Bedford* in No. 2 dock, completed in 1863, is a steamship with auxiliary sails furled on its foremast and boom. The building in the foreground with the patterned brick chimney houses the steam engines used for pumping water in and out of the two dry docks. On the far side of the dock there are no buildings and the presence of a large number of concrete blocks beside the railway line suggests that the dock may have only recently been completed. Its gate, or caisson, had been towed round from the foundry of Sandys, Vivian and Company at Hayle in October 1862 by the steamer *Queen*. As it was a fine day, about 300 people took the trip around Lands End which lasted ten hours and ended at 11.30 p.m. One building not shown is the lifeboat shed, erected just behind the *Bedford's* foremast in August 1867; the arrival of the town's first lifeboat, *City of Gloucester*, was delayed until the boathouse, shown on p. 68, was ready. Originally it had been planned to build a large floating dock or tidal basin for cargo handling on the far side of the western breakwater so that ships could stay afloat at all stages of the tide. The 80 ft wide entrance to this 14 acres of water was to be controlled by lock gates and the gap for these, known as 'the bridge', which was left in the breakwater can be seen behind the windjammer lying off the jetty. This basin was never built and all cargo handling was done alongside the breakwaters.

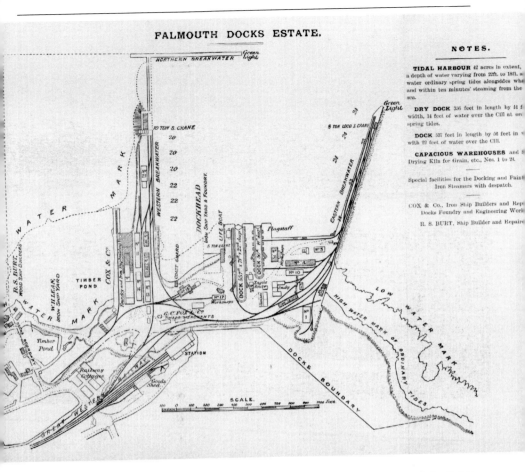

FALMOUTH DOCKS ESTATE.

NOTES.

TIDAL HARBOUR 42 acres in extent, a depth of water varying from 22ft. to 18ft. water ordinary spring tides alongside wha and within ten minutes' steaming from the sea.

DRY DOCK 356 feet in length by 14 f width, 14 feet of water over the Cill at or spring tides.

DOCK 537 feet in length by 56 feet in with 22 feet of water over the Cill.

CAPACIOUS WAREHOUSES and Drying Kiln for Grain, etc., Nos. 1 to 24.

Special facilities for the Docking and Paint Iron Steamers with despatch.

COX & Co., Iron Ship Builders and Repa Docks Foundry and Engineering Work

R. S. BURT, Ship Builder and Repaire

This map, taken from a brochure issued by 'Falmouth Docks (in possession of the Public Works Loan Commissioners)' and dated 1884, shows the layout of the whole Docks Estate up to 1914. In addition to the original pattern of breakwaters it shows the relative location of most of the features shown in the next few pages: the beach used for fish landings at the inland end of the western breakwater (p. 62) which was eventually the site of Nos 3 and 4 docks (pp. 70–72); the shallow water to the west of this breakwater which had to be extensively dredged before more jetties could be built on that side (p. 62); the relative size of the first two docks built and the pumphouse between them (p. 63); the railways on the breakwaters for loading and unloading cargoes (pp. 65 and 67); the lifeboat house (p. 68), and the shipbuilding area of Cox and Co. (p. 73). The original shape of the feature known as the Bar, before it was totally obliterated under successive reclamation schemes culminating in the Port Pendennis development, is clearly seen with its tide-mill and mill pond, here marked as 'timber pool' (p. 86). As early as 1863 the *West Briton* was able to report: 'There is at present full employ and constant demand for the wharves, stores, docks and other conveniences.' But thirty years later, at its half-yearly general meeting, the Company reported that work was slack, much of the china clay trade had been lost on account of an increase in railway rates, and the grain trade was increasing so that a large grain warehouse had recently been erected.

Up to the First World War the beach inside the tidal harbour was used largely for landing fish. Although Falmouth had no fishing fleet to speak of, boats from other ports landed fish caught near Falmouth on this beach. Several Penzance-registered boats are lying off the beach, landing boats are rowing out to collect their fish in barrels, and horse-carts are waiting to take the catch to the railway station. The Lowestoft fishing fleet used these facilities when fishing in western waters to get their catch to market quickly (see *Falmouth* p. 87).

This low tide view from the high ground of Trefusis Point shows the western part of the Docks and the Bar. The shipyards of Cox and Co. have ships on the stocks to the right of the western breakwater, and further to the right are the sheds of the Bar shipbuilders. Adjacent to the breakwater is the shallow promontory, known originally as Bar Point, and in the foreground *Princess Victoria* is returning from an excursion. In the background, left to right, may be seen the large roof of Falmouth railway station, the crescent of coastguard houses now known as Bay View Crescent, and the Falmouth Hotel with its square extension at the western end, enabling this picture to be dated post-1898. The large area of shallow water to the west of the breakwater was remembered as a particular hazard by Mr George Fox who used to travel on the six-oared gigs employed as boarding boats up to the 1850s which sometimes ran on to the mud and lost position, trying to cut corners, 'much to the amusement and chaffing of their rivals'.

This late-nineteenth-century scene in the two dry docks is typical of the activities in the yard by that time. The gate of the smaller No. 1 dock is closed, suggesting that the sailing vessel is undergoing repair, whereas No. 2 dock gate is open, the dock itself full of water, and it is likely the steamer is being taken out of dock, probably assisted by the tug whose bow can just be seen beyond her stern. It was not unusual for two ships to share a dock as it was not only cheaper but it meant less time waiting for repair. In spite of the gradual ascendency of steam over sail, the steamer, like that on p. 60, is 'sail assisted', having sails furled on its yards. The view of the windjammer's deck is interesting in that it illustrates one of the advantages of these vessels over the early steamers – their ability to carry much more cargo. Unencumbered with engines, the hull was a vast cargo-carrying space and the crew's living quarters were in the deckhouses clearly shown here. The sheds around the docks were used by businesses often independent of the Dock Company carrying on a number of activities from foundry work to grain storage. The general untidiness of the dockyard is noticeable, with timber, iron and odd pieces of equipment lying around the dockside, making it easy to understand why crew members returning to their ship after a night in the town's hostelries, often had accidents including falling into the dock.

This advertisement from Lake's *Almanac* of 1913 illustrates the way in which Falmouth Docks Company conducted its business. Its management board ran the organization on behalf of the Public Works Loan Commissioners, controlled the dry docks and cranes, supplied water and ballast, hired warehouse space and offered land to other businesses. All ship repairs were carried out by other firms which hired the dry docks, while other companies stored and distributed such imported commodities as coal, grain, oil cake (for cattle feed), timber and sacks. Shipbuilding and ship breaking were important activities and there were unloading facilities for fishing vessels (as shown on p. 62). The eastern breakwater was the recognized passenger terminal to Ireland and other Channel ports to the east. But all this was to change with the outbreak of the First World War. In addition to his duties in the Docks which had commenced in 1882, F.J. Bowles was an alderman of Falmouth Borough and mayor for five years in 1899, 1900 and 1909 to 1911, Justice of the Peace, a member of the Education Committee and governor of Falmouth Grammar School, Secretary of the Chamber of Commerce and of Church House, the religious and social society of Falmouth parish church, lay-reader at the Falmouth Mission Room (on the Moor), vice-president of Falmouth Unionist Association, president of the Central Guild of Help (a charitable organization for the needy people of the town), and a Borough Council representative on the Harbour Commissioners.

Soon after the railway arrived in Falmouth in 1863, broad gauge lines were laid into the Docks so that cargo could be brought in and taken away directly on the national rail network. One of the earliest commodities handled in this way was china clay brought from the St Austell area. Here, the *Susan Vittery* lies alongside the eastern breakwater ready to load its clay cargo from railway wagons using the mobile steam crane; the clay was usually taken to Runcorn and thence to the Potteries by canal. The *Susan Vittery* was lost at sea in 1953.

This Opie photograph shows some of the improvements made in the dockyard after the First World War. The lifeboat house has been replaced by a power station to generate the yard's electricity. The steamship in No. 2 dock looks altogether more modern than those shown in earlier pictures and does not have sails on its masts. But most indicative of the expansion brought about by the London firm of Green and Silley Weir, who took over the yard in 1918, is the large pile of concrete blocks in the foreground, no doubt associated with the new dry docks excavated during and after the war.

STEAM COMMUNICATION   FALMOUTH, PLYMOUTH,
BETWEEN   AND GUERNSEY.

THE

SIR F. DRAKE,

Of 110 Tons and 70 Horse-Power,

THOMAS WARD, COMMANDER,

LEAVES

Falmouth for Plymouth,

On Mondays and Wednesdays, at half-past 7 o'Clock in the Morning,

PLYMOUTH FOR GUERNSEY,

Every Thursday at 5 o'clock in the Afternoon, and leaves Guernsey the following day at the same hour; and

PLYMOUTH FOR FALMOUTH, EVERY TUESDAY & SATURDAY,

At 11 o'clock in the Forenoon,

Calling off Mevagissey, Wind and Weather permitting.

FARES BETWEEN FALMOUTH AND

	Chief Cabin.	Fore Cabin.
Plymouth	£0 12 6	£0 7 0
Mevagissey	0 5 0	0 3 0
Guernsey	1 10 6	0 18 0
Between Plymouth and Mevagissey	0 8 0	0 5 0

Deck Passengers between Plymouth and Guernsey, 6s.

A Female Attendant for the Ladies' Cabin.   Children under Ten Years of age, half-price.

	Horses.	Carriages per wheel.	Dogs.
Falmouth to Plymouth	£0 16 0	£0 7 6	2s. 0d.
Guernsey	2 0 0	1 0 0	5s. 0d.

Luggage and Merchandize carefully conveyed at reduced freights.

The LORD BERESFORD Steam Packet, leaves Guernsey for Jersey, after the arrival of the Sir F. DRAKE, which will enable Passengers to proceed to that place without loss of time; and the ARIADNE arrives at Guernsey from Jersey and St. Maloes, one hour before the departure of the Sir F. DRAKE.

The Proprietors of the Sir F. DRAKE have given her a new set of Boilers, with other desirable improvements in her Machinery, &c. which will ensure to Passengers, Expedition, Safety, and Comfort. If sufficient encouragement is given, she will run once a week through out the winter.

The Proprietors will not be liable for detention arising from accident; nor responsible for any Package or Luggage not booked by one of the Agents, or of the value of £5, unless paid for accordingly.

Passengers from Cornwall will be enabled to proceed twice a week from Plymouth to London, by the way of Portsmouth, by cheap and powerful Steam Vessels; particulars may be had at the principal Inns in Plymouth, Devonport, Stonehouse, and Falmouth, in Capt. WARD, on board, or the following Agents,

J. DIXON, *Falmouth.*   T. RUSSELL, *Stonehouse.*

W. JONES, *Guernsey.*

FALMOUTH: PRINTED BY T. P. DIXON, BOOKSELLER, &c.

This poster shows what the early steam-assisted sailing ships looked like and provides interesting information concerning the first steam ferries to call at Falmouth. *Sir Francis Drake* was a paddle steamer bought by a Falmouth captain, Thomas Ward, in 1829, which made two trips a week to Plymouth with a journey to the Channel Islands in between where it linked up with other island ferries. Passengers picked up at Mevagissey were brought out to the ferry by local boatmen and transferred at sea as she lay offshore. The service lasted until 1859 when the rail link to Truro was completed and the ferry was sold. The coastal ferry link was, however, maintained by the British and Irish Steam Packet Company on its journeys between Dublin and London and the *Lady Gwendolen*, 2,163 tons, seen below, was one of its six steamers calling twice weekly at Falmouth, Plymouth, Southampton, Portsmouth and London 'carrying cargo, passengers and livestock'.

Another of the steamers belonging to the British and Irish Steam Packet Company was *Lady Wolseley*, seen here alongside the eastern breakwater which was the ferry terminal. *Lady Wolseley* was a regular and familiar visitor to the port, but on the afternoon of Tuesday 20 August 1906, the tug *Marion* was on her way back from Dartmouth when she ran into fog off Start Point and after groping her way down the coast, hailed a fishing boat which told her she was in Gerrans Bay. Soon afterwards the sound of a large ship's hooter was heard and a steamer came out of the fog heading straight for *Marion* which had to take rapid evasive action to avoid being run down. 'Land right ahead' shouted Captain Mitchell and immediately the steamer's engines were put into reverse, but when *Marion* reached her *Lady Wolseley* was fast on the rocks near Killigerran Head. Attempts to tow her off on the falling tide failed and *Marion* was soon joined by *Victor* with Falmouth lifeboat in tow, Gerrans Coastguard having informed Falmouth of the situation using the newly established coastal telephone. The passenger-tug took off about 150 people and then returned to the stranded vessel. Those left on board were assured by Captain Black that they were in no danger, and after a piano was brought on deck a sing-song was organized. At low tide during the night the ship's officers and Mr Carne, the agent, examined the position of the vessel and discovered that, by sheer good fortune, the hull had missed the jagged rocks of the headland and grounded on a smooth patch of rock. At high tide next morning the tugs *Victor*, *Marion* and *Queen of the Fal* attached hawsers and successfully pulled *Lady Wolseley* off the rocks and slowly escorted her to the eastern breakwater. At 1.35 p.m. her journey to Ireland was continued, none the worse for the experience which the *Falmouth Packet* described later as 'an undesirable acquaintance with the rock-bound coast of Cornwall', and claimed was the result of compass error brought about by a cargo of 50 tons of steel girders stowed on the deck just below the compass.

Another of the old 'wooden walls' to end her days in Falmouth after the Royal Navy had converted to steam-driven ships was HMS *St Vincent*. She is seen in 1906 in No. 2 dock in process of being broken up: the top deck and foremast have been removed and there is a pile of wood on the dockside. Much of the panelling from the captain's quarters and some of the doors were used in the Seamen's Bethel in Quay Hill (p. 98). The dry dock would have been hired from the Docks Company for this purpose, although other vessels would have continued to use it, as the steamer astern shows. The lifeboat house shows up clearly to the left of *St Vincent's* mast. One of the ship's anchors (below) was presented to the town and placed in an enclosure behind Gyllyngvase Beach with a suitable plaque and this served as an added entertainment for children on the beach who used it as a slide until its removal for scrap as part of the town's salvage drive during the Second World War.

The Anchor, Falmouth Beach

During the First World War the function of Falmouth Docks changed after the Admiralty took over the yard in 1914. Repairs to war-damaged ships became the first priority, especially after the launching of the German submarine offensive in 1915. Among the more unusual visitors were the steamships *Iris* and *Daffodil*, former Mersey ferryboats which had been severely damaged in what was regarded as the first-ever 'combined operations' raid on Zeebrugge in Belgium. The Germans used the canal there as a submarine base and the raid on 23 April 1918 was intended to sink blockships (old cruisers filled with concrete) in the canal entrance, while the cruiser *Vindictive*, with *Iris* and *Daffodil* in support as landing ships, attacked the $1\frac{1}{2}$-mile mole (jetty) which protected the canal entrance. The venture was only partially successful and casualties were heavy, *Iris* returning with 77 dead and 105 wounded aboard. While in Falmouth undergoing repair, the two vessels were opened to visitors and these pictures were taken on that occasion.

SS *DAFFODIL* MAY 12th 1918 AFTER ZEBRUGGE

The view above can be dated to about 1910 as the large 'mansions' along Trefusis Road, Flushing appear newly built; the western breakwater has its old grain sheds, and the expanse of water in the foreground, the fish landing beach on p. 62, was not to survive the war. Soon after the outbreak of war, after the Admiralty had assumed control of the yard, the volume of ship repair work increased so much that, by 1917, it was far beyond the capacity of the local workforce and facilities, and a London firm, R.H. Green and Silley Weir, was directed by the Admiralty to investigate the situation. After an inspection of the dockyard, the first step was to send from London a contingent of skilled workmen whose priority task was to streamline the repair operation to keep pace with the arrival of vessels needing repair. The Admiralty had already decided to construct a third, larger dry dock in the area shown above, adjacent to No. 2 dock, but wartime delays meant that plans drawn up in 1916 were not implemented until 1918, when construction work was

begun. The seaward end of the dock had to be built out into tidal water and wooden jetties were built to carry the cranes responsible for placing the massive concrete blocks required (opposite). A special vessel, SS *City of York*, was chartered by the builders, G. Shellabear and Son of Plymouth, to carry much of the necessary raw material such as river sand, pump-dredged from the Ruan River in the upper reaches of the Fal estuary, concrete blocks from Penryn quay (often towing flat barges carrying more blocks), and enormous quantities of crushed stone from the Porthoustock quarries across the bay. The picture above shows the final stages of construction in full swing in December 1920, with the stepped concrete sides of the dock almost complete and six steam cranes in action. On the right a steam locomotive is towing trucks probably full of the rock chippings which it appears to be dumping into the dock to make the thick layer of concrete for the dock floor which is being laid in the foreground. The dam erected at the seaward end to keep out the water was eventually replaced with a pair of hinged gates. On the extreme left can be seen the bedrock from which the inland end of the dock had to be excavated and which has been carved into steps to match the concrete blocks further along. The new dock was finally opened in 1921 and became one of the largest in Great Britain at that time (see *Falmouth* p. 91). In the course of its wartime association with Falmouth, the firm of Green and Silley Weir had realized the enormous potential of the Falmouth yard and so, after lengthy negotiations with the Public Works Loan Commissioners, Falmouth Docks Company and Cox and Co., the whole enterprise passed into single ownership in 1918 and became known, eventually, as Silley Cox and Company Ltd.

The expansion and development of Falmouth Docks continued into the 1920s with the excavation of a fourth dry dock, parallel to No. 3 but not so large. Begun in 1924 and opened in 1928, the construction of this dock is seen in the picture above with seven steam cranes engaged in lifting, excavating and pile-driving. The busy locomotive in the foreground is taking excavated material to be dumped in the Bar creek and pool which was filled in as the first step in the total disappearance of this historic area. The picture below shows the seaward end of the same dock with the gates open as the tugs bring out the *Cutty Sark* prior to her departure in 1938.

In the late 1860s the brothers Joseph Goodenough Cox and Herbert Henry Cox set up in business as ship's chandlers in Falmouth. The business expanded with the growth in ship repairing to include a smithy and forge, after which a new site for the business was established on the land shown here to the west of the western breakwater under the name of the Docks, Foundry and Engineering Company and, later Cox and Co., Engineers. It was not long before the company began to build ships here, the first being *Lizard* in 1878. In spite of the 1918 reorganization, shipbuilding went on until 1930, by which time 198 vessels had been launched, including many of the passenger-tugs working in the harbour and described elsewhere in this book. The last vessels to be built here were six large trawlers for French owners to fish on the Newfoundland Banks. At the time, these vessels were the largest trawlers in the world – over 213 ft in length and 1,450 tons, with a maximum speed of 14 knots. One of them, *Spitzbergen*, is seen here at anchor in the harbour during trials.

Not long after the construction of No. 4 dock, the Company set about extending the wharfage space: the eastern and western breakwaters had been lengthened in 1923 and the northern arm rebuilt and lengthened in 1926–8. After the shallow water between the western breakwater and the town had been dredged, further jetties were built: the first of these, built 1931–3, is shown above with a single boat alongside. To forge stronger links with Australia and to reduce the expenditure of US dollars, it had been decided to use timber from Queensland and the SS *Belpareil* was unloading 5,000 turpentine piles over 70 ft long, each weighing about 8 tons. Because of this, the *Western Morning News* reported in February 1932, that it was to be named the Empire Wharf. Later, the King's Wharf was built, nearer to the Bar (1935–7), and the westward extension of the northern arm, named the Queen's Wharf, between 1938 and 1942 (see p. 80).

A feature of the harbour scene up to the 1950s was this steam-powered floating crane *Titania* which became a weathercock to all harbour users as the jib always pointed away from the wind. The Dutch-built crane was captained by Bert See, with Tommy Tregidgo as mate and Will Bird crane operator. Employed in lifting very heavy weights such as the large concrete blocks used in building the new docks, and ships' boilers, she was kept up at Tolverne during the war as she was a landmark for enemy bombers while anchored in the harbour.

During the Second World War the Docks came under the control of the Admiralty again. In mid-1940, following the German invasion of France and the evacuation of allied troops from Europe, the port was filled with ships of all the nations occupied by the Germans. To boost morale, especially after the air raids which the port endured in the years after 1940, Their Majesties King George VI and Queen Elizabeth visited the town and were conducted over the Docks by Mr H.A.J. Silley (above), watched by a respectful work-force. The picture below shows the royal party crossing one of the dock gates, here accompanied by Mr Silley (bowler hat), Mr George Green (hatless, left) and Mr Robert Smeaton, General Manager (extreme right). The vessel whose funnel is in the background is the *Registan*, under repair in the Docks having been attacked in the Irish Sea in May 1941.

The call for a 'second front', an invasion of the mainland of Europe, became increasingly strident after the American entry into the war. Positive plans began to take shape from mid-1943 onwards and the whole Fal estuary became an important part of the build-up of men and materials. A large hutted camp called the US Navy Advanced Amphibious Base (see *Falmouth* p. 148) was set up on the Beacon to accommodate our visiting allies and operational facilities were set up in the Docks. Grove Place (p. 93) was converted into a repair and maintenance base and several sea-front hotels were taken over for administrative and medical purposes. The picture above shows one of the many large landing craft being towed by *Northgate Scot* towards the dry docks with the western breakwater and Falmouth town in the background. Of the many unusual-looking vessels forming part of the invasion fleet, none were more peculiar than the units of the Mulberry harbour (opposite, below) which were towed over to Normandy to build a breakwater and harbour after the initial invasion had established a bridgehead. Several of these units were kept in the Helford River prior to their departure. The scene alongside the eastern breakwater above contains two different types of invasion craft, the nearer is LCT124 with its large bow-door for carrying and landing tanks. Away from the town itself, most of the estuary was used in some way to prepare for the D-Day invasion and King Harry Reach, Turnaware and Tolverne witnessed a great build-up of assault craft. New roads were made down to the waterside in several places by US engineers to enable large lorries and tanks to embark directly on to the ships and these still afford access to the shores of the beautiful Fal river today. After a week of frantic embarkation activity in June 1944, all seemed quiet after

their departure with only supply and maintenance troops left behind. To commemorate their stay in Falmouth the US naval personnel presented to the town a shelter, erected on the sea front, with a suitably engraved plaque set in the floor (see *Falmouth* p. 150).

The post-war shipping boom meant continuous work for the dockyard and, at its peak, over 3,000 men were employed. The management board, aware of the trend towards bigger oil tankers at that time, decided in 1952 to inaugurate an expansion plan. By 1954 new BP tankers of 32,000 tons had reached the limit of the dry docks' capacity, and as even larger vessels were planned, up to 65,000 tons, it was decided to enlarge No. 2 dock. The entrance was built out into the tidal water as far as possible to allow vessels to be lined up without hitting the northern arm; at the inland end the 110 ft cliff had to be taken back 50 yards which involved moving the Castle Drive road on the cliff top and the main town sewer below and the removal of a quarter of a million cubic yards of rock in 1956–7. The widening and lengthening of the dock itself was mostly into solid rock and the thirty thousand cubic yards of material removed was used to reclaim land on the east side of the Docks Estate. In the picture work is well advanced on the left although much rock has to be excavated on the right. The plant on the dock floor is making cement which is being taken away by the dumper trucks in the foreground. Although the nature of the work was somewhat different, it is interesting to compare the technique and equipment used here with those for the initial construction of Nos 3 and 4 docks (pp. 70–2). Some of the small steam cranes appear still to be in use. In May 1958 the new dock was

opened by HRH Prince Philip, Duke of Edinburgh, who named the installation the Queen Elizabeth Dock as he unveiled the plaque seen in the picture below. The dock was 850 ft long, 136 ft wide, 36 ft deep, and capable of taking ships up to 85,000 tons, but the first vessel did not enter until September as much of the equipment had to be installed after the naming ceremony. Unfortunately, during the years it had taken to build the new dock, the size of oil tankers had increased enormously as the age of the VLCC (very large crude carrier) had arrived and, before long, tankers up to 200,000 tons were sailing the oceans of the world and the plans to make Falmouth the world's tanker repair centre rapidly evaporated.

This aerial photograph of the early 1950s shows how the shortage of both wharfage and dry dock capacity after the war was overcome. In the centre foreground can be seen the beginnings of the construction of two new wharves to the west of the Docks Estate on the land formerly used by the shipbuilders Cox and Co. up to the 1930s. Pile-driving and dredging went on for several years to create new deep water berths, and when the concrete deck had been laid they were named the Duchy (parallel to the King's Wharf) and County Wharves, opened in 1956. Alongside the Empire and King's Wharves are the two large, box-like floating docks which increased by fifty per cent the graving capacity of the yard. But, sadly, this happy situation was short-lived: by the early 1960s the Docks began to suffer from the general world decline in shipping and ten years later, Silley Cox was superseded by P&O, soon after which the yard was nationalized and became part of British Shipbuilders. The absolute nadir was reached in 1979 when the yard was closed completely for several months, after which it reopened with a much reduced work-force. The prosperous days of this picture were never to be seen again.

The beautiful barque *Pamir* lies alongside the County Wharf, watched by a young Gordon Bullen with his Maypole delivery bike. This may well have been the last time this gracious windjammer visited Falmouth before she was lost in Atlantic hurricane 'Carrie' in September 1957, 600 miles off the Azores. Eighty-one persons went down with her, despite the fact that she had been fitted with an auxiliary engine which some said was partly to blame for her loss. In her fifty-year lifetime, this 4,200-ton iron vessel made many journeys from Australia with grain, her fastest being 96 days in 1939 and her last in 1949, 127 days from Port Victoria. During the heyday of 'Falmouth for Orders' hundreds of large sailing ships had come to the port, but it was not the only port used for that purpose. Under certain weather conditions incoming vessels found it easier to call at Cork for their orders especially during a long spell of wind from between east and north. But a strong advocate of Falmouth as the better destination was the *Commercial Herald* of San Francisco which extolled Falmouth although a majority of departures from the American port were bound for Cork. Falmouth, the *Herald* alleged, was better because, of the 165 wheat-laden vessels to leave San Francisco in 1873, 117 went on to ports east of Falmouth. Although Cork claimed that most of the vessels went to northern ports, this had been proved wrong. Furthermore, the establishment of the Lizard Signal Station, which 'spoke' to vessels by flag signals to discover name and destination so that the owner could be informed by electric telegraph, was much appreciated by both ship owners and receivers of cargo. All this made Falmouth the better destination.

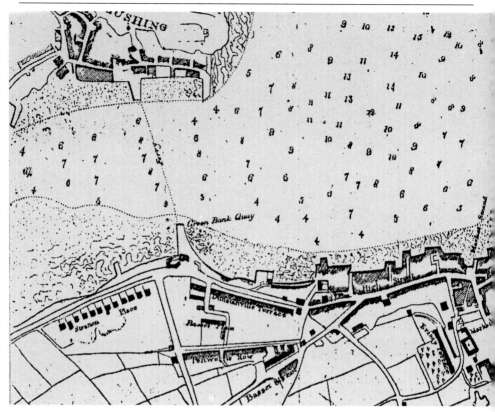

Richard Thomas (1779–1858) was a civil engineer whose extensive knowledge of Cornwall, especially that part around Falmouth, which he made his home, persuaded him to write a *Falmouth Guide* in 1815, published by Lake and Co. In 1827 he wrote a *History of Falmouth*, published by Trathan. This map, surveyed and drawn by him to accompany the book, clearly shows how small the built-up part of the town was at that time, although most of the street plan already exists. To the south of the Pier, the name given to Custom House Quay, there was little development and the Manor House of Arwenack looked out over the waters of the harbour. Beside it, a grove of elm trees with the Killigrew monument in its centre stands on the site of the present Grove Place. The distinctive shape of the Bar as it was originally is shown clearly with its tide-mill and pool which, with other pools in the vicinity, was used for seasoning the timber used in the ship-building yards which covered much of its area. Inland of the Bar are Cromwell's Entrenchments, ditches dug by the Commonwealth forces besieging Pendennis Castle in 1646. The Avenue or Ropewalk extended further up the hill to join Bar Lane, the present Melvill Road, roughly at the end of what is now Lansdowne Road. The name 'Bank' shown running along the seaward side of the Grove was simply the bank or shore of the harbour and this name is retained today in Bank Place and Bank House, the latter built by Robert Were Fox in 1788. The complex of quays called The Pier has changed little since it was built by the second Peter Killigrew in the 1670s except that the seaward arm of the southern pier was doubled in width in 1903. The reason for the sharp double bend at the junction of Church Street and Arwenack Street, known today as Church Corner, is shown clearly by the existence of an inlet known as Harvey's Dock. There are no piers at Fish

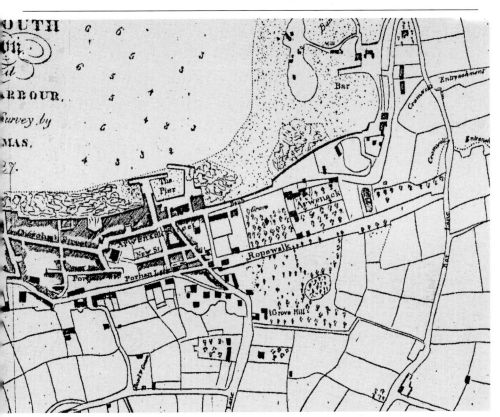

Strand or Market Strand; at the latter, tidal water reached as far as the road until a stone pier was built in 1871 (p. 107). Between High Street, once known as Ludgate Hill, and the harbour a number of 'opes' allowed access to tidal water for those men whose work was connected with the sea. Once a busy working area concerned entirely with harbour-related activities, it has recently become almost entirely residential. In front of Dunstanville Terrace, better known today as Greenbank, was part of the commercial waterfront, the quay now occupied by the Royal Cornwall Yacht Club having been a coal yard. The present Greenbank Gardens, made as recently as 1913, was covered with work-shops and workmen's yards occupied by Olver and Sons, among others, who built St Anthony Lighthouse in 1834–5. The most striking feature of this map is the essentially waterfront situation of the town in 1827. Much of today's town area was then occupied by agricultural land belonging to a number of farms which have disappeared, although some of the farmhouses still exist. The most notable exception to this is the valley stretching inland westward to include the Market Place, known today as the Moor, where the Market House was built in 1812. Buildings were springing up along Berkeley Place and the lower part of Killigrew Street. Also of interest here is the existence of two quarries from which much of the building stone was obtained for the older part of the town; as the built-up area expanded after this date not only was the quarry above Berkeley Place con-siderably enlarged to become today's Town Quarry but quarries in other parts of the growing town were opened up. Another area of development away from the waterfront was along the road which led out to Swanpool, shown on the map as Wood Lane.

These two photographs are a panoramic pair showing the inner harbour and waterfront at a date between 1878 and 1890, evidenced by the absence of the Submarine Pier, built 1890, and the presence of the Trevethan Board School clock tower, built 1878. Many other features of historical interest are portrayed and a careful study gives an excellent impression of Falmouth in the 1880s. In the immediate foreground is the original Falmouth railway station with the roof over the passenger platforms, the chimneys of the ancillary buildings on the right and the large goods shed on the left. The 'stature' of the trucks beside this shed, as well as the distinctive appearance of the railway lines, indicate that this was part of the broad gauge railway which was changed to standard gauge in 1892. The Docks buildings beyond the station roof are the warehouses and sheds of the Docks Company, although the buildings on the extreme left (with the chimneys) carry the nameboard of Cox and Company, Shipbuilders. To the right of these sheds the internal railway curves round behind the beach on to the western breakwater. Several interesting features on the Bar include the baulks of timber resting on the mud which are being seasoned by the sea water as the tide rises and falls, the defunct tide-mill standing on its barrier-like wall which originally enclosed the mill-pool, a large two-masted vessel to the left of the mill showing how far tidal water rises in the Bar Creek, and the group of sheds on the curving projection of the Bar to the right of the mill which, according to Lake's

Directory of 1895, are Harvey's timber yard and the shipyards of Symonds and Burt. The inner part of the Bar does not show up clearly on this picture and details of it are better seen on pp. 88–9, although Penwennack, the large building to the right of the railway bridge, stands out and is a private house which later became a hotel; immediately to its right is the chimney of W.H. Lean's boatyard. On the town side of the Bar, the Killigrew monument stands out clearly on Arwenack Green in front of the Manor House, and further right are the majestic terrace of Grove Place, Bank House, at this date a biscuit factory and coal yard of the Downing family, and Bank Place, with a flagstaff in front of the Sailors' Home and Hospital, established here in 1852. Across the road from these buildings is the tidal water of the Grove Place beach, at the far end of which is a hulk used as a dry dock for many years for the repair of small vessels. The large building behind the hulk is Commercial Buildings. Stretching into the distance along the shore of the Penryn river, past Custom House Quay, the more prominent features are the gasworks and chimneys, Market Strand Pier, Pye's Cellars, Well Beach, the Royal Cornwall Yacht Club and the Greenbank Hotel with its white-painted quay. Across the water, little can be seen of Flushing except for the engine house of the abandoned Clinton Mine on top of the cliff, above the Docks sheds (see *Falmouth* p. 117). None of the large mansions which now decorate this section of coastline has yet been built.

This close-up view of the tide-mill on the Bar shows further deterioration, and the structure was eventually demolished in 1914. High tide has filled the mill-pool through the
sluices seen beside the mill, and beyond that a topsail schooner is in Burt's shipbuilding
yard, one of five such yards in this area at the time.

In the background of this picture of Bar Creek at high tide stands Tower House with its
distinctive structure on the roof, only removed during the Second World War after nearby
bombing had weakened its structure. To its right are the houses of Bar Terrace and in
front of them, on the opposite side of the road, the 'split level' buildings with only one
storey on the road side but with two floors at the rear, the lower level being used as storage sheds for the businesses around the creek. The view is dominated by the steam-engine
chimney of W.H. Lean's shipyard where many wooden and, later, iron vessels were built
up to 1926. Lean's yard had suffered a disastrous fire in August 1880, when the pitch-
covered wooden sheds were destroyed, together with the adjacent Redruth Brewery depot;
the Dock Hotel and stables were only saved by the exertions of the Garrison and
Volunteer Fire Brigades.

The tidal beach on the outer side of the Bar was used for repairing ships, and here the large, three-masted schooner *Fanny Crossfield* stands high and dry in, probably, Burt's yard. This old family firm was long established on this site up to the mid-1920s and was advertised in successive editions of Lake's *Directory* as 'Ship, Yacht and Launch Builder'. *Fanny Crossfield* was one of the fleet of schooners operated by James Fisher and Sons of Barrow. In its seventy years of existence between the 1850s and the 1920s this company was concerned mainly with the smelting business of the north-east and the coal trade. Its 130 vessels made it the largest fleet of merchant schooners to have operated for any British company. In the background the Submarine Pier and Grove Place can be seen.

This 1880s photograph of the northern end of the Bar shows the curving road which formed the boundary of this commercial and industrial area. The slope in the foreground was to become the gardens of the houses in Bar Terrace when they were built a few years later. On the far side of the road are the sheds of 'Willmore: Corn, Flour and Salt Merchant'. The Arthur Willmore business, founded in 1793, also had a shop at 47 Church Street. Further along to the right was a lime-kiln and brick and tile store whose proprietor, R.A. Newcombe, lived in Penryn, and next to it was Lime Kiln Cottage, home of the lime-burner, Sampson H. Pascoe. On the far side of these sheds is the tidal water of Bar Creek with a laden topsail schooner alongside the end of the Bar at Symonds' Yard. The hulk to the left of this vessel is on the edge of the shipbuilding yard of H.S. Trethowan which spread back to the road on the extreme left where a white signboard is visible through the branches of a tree. This large, busy yard built and repaired many vessels up to 1892 when it was sold to the War Department who built barracks for the

Falmouth Volunteer Division of the Submarine Miners, Royal Engineers. In 1890 a pier was built from this site, projecting 395 ft into the harbour from beside the Killigrew Obelisk on Arwenack Green. This became known as the Submarine Pier and was used by the *General Elliott* (p. 90), the steamer used to lay the electrically-detonated mines on the sea floor in the harbour entrance in case of enemy attack. An 18 in gauge railway line was laid from the barracks to the end of the pier where there was a crane. The mine-laying procedure entailed the use of six to eight quay punts whose owners were volunteer members of the detachment. The barracks had been built by March 1892 and the move from Arwenack completed. Soon after the barracks had been built the Volunteer Regiment was disbanded and replaced by a militia force of part-time soldiers who trained for up to three months each year. Stretching away behind Trethowan's sheds are Grove Place and Bank Place, better seen on later pages.

After the Submarine Miners Militia had replaced the Volunteers in 1893 few of the officers were local men. This group, pictured in 1897 in the Barracks, shows, standing, left to right: Lieut. H.C. Fanshawe, Major Baskerville (commandant), Capt. G.L. Fanshawe RE (Adjutant), Lieut. Wainwright. Sitting: Capt. and Hon. Major Johnson, Capt. and Hon. Major Prower, Lieut. D'Arcy Hutton, Lieut. Vyvyan, Lieut. Sugg RE (coast battalion).

The Submarine Miners' steamer *General Elliott* is on its way out to the harbour entrance with its mines slung alongside, ready for laying on the sea floor after being connected to the electric cables whose ends were attached to buoys. *General Elliott* arrived in the port in September 1889, straight from the Heard and Barnard shipyard in Hull, already fitted with derricks on the masts and at the bow. A skilled local seaman, W.R. Richards, was master of the vessel until his retirement in 1906.

These similar views of the whole Bar area were photographed some years either side of 1890 as the Submarine Pier shown below is absent on the very detailed picture above. In this older view, showing the extensive exposure of mud at low tide, the tide-mill and the quay behind the Dock and Railway Inn stand out clearly. Below the curving road of the Castle Drive, the large railway station building dominates the left of the picture, while in front of the station an iron steam ship is being built in the yard of Cox and Co. Other vessels lie on the beach on the outside of the Bar. On the extreme right two wooden ships stand on the stocks in W.H. Lean's yard next to the Dock and Railway Inn. The broader view below shows several changes to the buildings on the outside of the Bar. In the foreground the masts of two topsail schooners lying alongside the Town Quay show above the surrounding buildings.

Two views along Grove Place in opposite directions. Above, the Killigrew Obelisk is surrounded by a wooded, fenced enclosure and the landward end of the Submarine Pier with its 18 in gauge railway is in the foreground. The high tide scene below shows water reaching the road and the fine terrace of houses in Grove Place (see *Falmouth* p. 103). At the end of the houses is Ingram Hall, built originally as a studio and art gallery for the well known local artist, William Ayerst Ingram, who arrived in Falmouth in the early 1890s and remained until his death in 1913. The gallery was used to stage exhibitions by several artists, including Henry Scott Tuke. More recently, Ingram Hall was used for a variety of purposes including a school canteen, before its demolition soon after the Second World War.

Two widely differing uses of the Grove Place beach. Above, the ketch *Eclipse* stands on the beach in August 1930. Built in Penryn in 1892, this 32-ton vessel came into the Morrison family in 1931 and was worked by Norman and his son Jimmy as a 'stone barge', carrying roadstone from the quarries at Porthoustock to destinations throughout the Helford and Fal estuaries, as far up as Gweek and Tresillian. Navigation along these tidal creeks was far from easy and local marks such as gates, trees and houses were used to keep to the winding navigable channel – but, occasionally, the vessel did run aground. Although commodities such as coal and agricultural produce were carried, stone was the main cargo and often sixty tons would be unloaded in three hours to enable the boat to catch the tide before it dropped too far to make the journey downstream. Increasing use of road transport put an end to this traffic and *Eclipse* was cut down to the waterline at the eastern end of Grove Place and eventually covered with several feet of mud until excavations off Trago Mills brought fragments of her to the surface. In 1943–4 the new Grove Place beach (left), further seaward after the dumping of Docks waste alongside the road, is used for the smaller landing craft and assault ships of the US Navy being made ready for the June 1944 invasion of France.

The quays built by the second Peter Killigrew in the 1670s have remained in constant use since then. They have been a safe, if temporary, refuge for visiting fishing vessels on a Sunday – Cornish fishermen never cast their nets on the Sabbath – or a base from which replenishment of water and provisions could be made. There were at one time seven public houses within a hundred yards of this quay. Many of the visiting fishermen took advantage of the facilities for worship offered by the Seamen's Bethel (pp. 98–9) and many boats would leave the basin flying the Bethel flag. In this picture, part of the St Ives fishing fleet is preparing to put to sea at high tide (See *Falmouth* p. 104).

Up to the First World War among the most regular users of these quays was the large number of sailing 'quay punts' which regularly went out beyond the Lizard to 'speak' to incoming square-riggers to obtain employment tending that vessel as long as it remained in port. Such vessels would stay at sea for several days, and the inhabitants of the Lizard complained frequently, as in the *West Briton* of 19 September 1872, that, 'We Lizard folks have been for many years sadly pestered by the pilfering of our gardens and orchards. The culprits are suspected to be the crews of sloops which sail from Falmouth to watch for home-bound vessels in the Channel.' Many stories are told of the rivalries between the family-owners of these hardy sailing boats. The quay punt *ICU*, owned by the Morrison family and said to have been named after the identification signal used at sea, is seen carrying plenty of sail against a background of the northern end of Falmouth town.

The sheltered water of the Custom House Quay basin was used by surprisingly large ketches and schooners to unload cargo. Here, the ketch *Emma* is unloading what is probably roadstone for making or repairing the town's highways: the stone is lifted out in a basket controlled by the man balanced precariously on the plank overlapping the boat and loaded into a wheelbarrow on the quayside. In the background is one of the several public houses around or near the quay; together with the Marine, shown here, the Globe, Ship, Quay, Dolphin, Oddfellows and Commercial were all nearby as well as two 'temperance hotels', the Lifeboat and Devon and Cornwall. Arwenack Street, that part of the town's main thoroughfare immediately behind these quays, catered for the other needs of ships in the basin: in addition to the varied provision shops, there were the three shipping agents, Fox, Broad, and Lashbrooke and Hunt, together with the harbourmaster, Pilots' Association, Board of Trade Surveyor, Deeble's (ships chandler and tug owner), George Rickard (blockmaker), the Mercantile Marine Club, three ships chandlers, and many of the watermen whose small boats performed the many and varied tasks of a working harbour in those days lived in Quay Hill.

Watermen Bye-Laws.

BOATMEN duly licensed and plying for hire, are entitled to the following fares in districts Nos. 2 and 3 for *one* to *three* passengers, and district No. 1 for *one* passenger only; every extra person to pay *half fare*.

Stations	Green Bank	Flushing.	Market Strand	Fish Strand and Custom House Quay	Penryn	District 1	District 2	District 3
Green Bank ...		3d.	4d.	6d.	1s.	1s.	3s.	4s.
Flushing	3d.		4d.	6d.	1s.	1s.	3s.	4s.
Market Strand ...		4d.		3d.	1s. 6d.	1s.	3s.	4s.
Fish Strand or Customs Quay...		6d.	3d.		1s. 6d.	1s.	3s.	4s.

DISTRICT NO. 1.—Within a straight line drawn from Trefusis Point to the end of the Eastern Breakwater of the Docks.

DISTRICT NO. 2.—Within straight lines drawn from Pendennis Point to St. Mawes Castle Point. and continued from thence to Pennarrow Point.

DISTRICT NO. 3.—Any place beyond the limits of No. 2, to the extent of the jurisdiction of the Harbour Commissioners for levying tolls. Beyond No. 3 and to their extent, the fare to be a matter of special agreement.

FARES FOR TIME.—Punt with two paddles, 1s. per hour ; sailing punts, 2s. per hour. When the number exceeds *six*, each passenger shall pay *fourpence* per hour. These fares are calculated for one to three passengers. One minute for every penny fare shall be allowed for waiting time, and no charge shall be made for children under *four* years of age. If above four and under *twelve* years of age, not more than half-fare may be charged.

FOR ADDITIONAL PASSENGERS.—When the fare is 3d. to 6d., *one-penny*; 6d. to .1s., *two-pence*; 1s. to 2s., *three-pence*; 2s. to 3s., *five-pence*; exceeding 3s., *six-pence*.

When the hiring during the day extends into night, *sixpence* per hour or part of hour extra for such time must be paid ; the night fare one-half more than ordinary, commencing at 9 o'clock p.m. and ends at 5 o'clock a.m., between March 31st and September 30th, and 6 p.m. and 6 a.m. for the remaining months. but at all times between midnight and 4 a.m. shall be double the day fares. *Back fares* will be *one-third* of the ordinary fare. Luggage of the weight of 56 lbs. will be allowed, but 3d. for each additional *half cwt.* or fraction thereof.

No boatman may refuse a fare without reasonable grounds for so doing—and the hirer shall be at liberty to prevent any other person from being a passenger with him.

Water Distances from Market Strand Pier.

To Penryn	1 mile 4 fur.	To Malpas	7 miles 6 fur.
,, Flushing Old Quay ...	0 ,, 4 ,,	,, Truro	9 ,, 5 ,,
,, Mylor Pier	2 ,, 3 ,,	,, St. Mawes Quay ...	2 ,, 5 ,,
,, Perran Wharf	6 ,, 2 ,,	,, Lizard	20 ,, 0 ,,
,, Turnaware	4 ,, 0 ,,	,, Goverack	11 ,, 1 ,,
,, Tregothnan Boat House	6 ,, 2 ,,	,, Helford Haven ...	5 ,, 6 ,,

This extract from the booklet of bye-laws published by Falmouth Borough Council in the 1890s lays down the regulations and scale of charges for the licensed watermen of the harbour. It is an attempt to regulate an otherwise undisciplined and unruly group of men whose activities and conduct in the harbour and on the piers led to numerous complaints in the local newspapers. The waterman's was a hard and precarious existence carried on in the worst of weathers, and it is surprising that there is no mention in this table of charges of their being allowed to charge double fare in rough weather. But here arose a problem: who was to decide when the weather could officially be classed as 'rough'? It was agreed that the harbourmaster should raise a flag on the flagstaff which stood outside his office, but he often forgot to do it which caused the watermen to complain. Then the task was given to the Coastguard, which at that time was stationed at the barracks at the top of High Street, but when the Coastguard moved to new premises at what is now Bay View Crescent the problem arose again and was never satisfactorily resolved.

'The Mission Cutter *Sickle* at work in Falmouth roadstead.' This sketch was drawn to accompany the 1888 report of the Missions to Seamen which tells us 'Falmouth Roads' was first occupied by the Missions to Seamen in 1861 and then goes on to say: 'The increase of steam-boats and the gradual diminishing of freights, consequent on bad trade, forcing shipowners to order their vessels to ports of discharge direct, instead of calling for orders, has greatly reduced the number of vessels entering Falmouth Roads. Still, the 3,700 craft which put into our harbour during the year 1888, including about 1,000 windbound, supplied abundant work for the work of our Mission, and there is every prospect of a large number of vessels calling for orders during the coming year. The mission-yacht has been out six days a week as usual and has borne us to many vessels in all kinds of weather. Divine service has been held on board the several English ships, week-days and Sundays, at which many thousand heard the Gospel. . . . One hundred and thirty seamen signed the total abstinence pledge and twelve joined the Shipwrecked Mariners' Society. One captain joined the ranks of the Mission helpers and two young men became Missions to Seamen Associates. It may be truly said that every year our duties become easier from the fact of an increasing knowledge amongst seamen of all nations of the aims and efforts of the Missions to Seamen. We are made as welcome on foreign vessels as on English and no sectarian barriers, except in a very few instances, are now set up against us. It is especially encouraging to find that our visits are often looked forward to with such real pleasure that it would evidently be a great disappointment to many sailors if their ships left the harbour without having had a service on board. There is no doubt a sad amount of crass indifference on board ship, especially among English seamen, but over against this we can set the bright and hopeful fact that large numbers of men are receiving the Word with all readiness of heart . . . and that thousands of men value and love our Mission Services who lately would be found in the dancing saloon and the public house. Statistics for the year 1888: 3,709 ships entered the harbour (including 1,170 for orders); paid 2,681 visits to ships, barges and fishing boats at Falmouth, Malpas and Truro; held 426 services afloat and 80 readings ashore: sold 139 Bibles and New Testaments and 22 Prayer Books; issued 91 bags of books; enrolled 1 Mission helper; 2 associates and 130 temperance men.'

The Seamen's Bethel was set up in Falmouth after a public meeting in May 1820, and a room was provided by the Seamen's Friend Society in Mulberry Square. In 1849 the Bethel moved to the old Watch House on North Quay, then into an old sail-loft nearby which was enlarged in 1851 and where it continued to operate under a succession of men whose names became legendary all over the world. These pictures show different views of the chapel: that above dates between 1916 and 1919 when Mr Noble (right) was missionary, accompanied by his co-worker, Mr W. Fenton. The picture below shows the unique

ship's bow pulpit for which the Bethel was best known, fitted with port and starboard lights and dedicated to the memory of King Edward VII; also prominent is the two-manual pipe organ presented by Mrs Davey to replace the old harmonium (see *Falmouth* pp. 109–10). As much of the missionary work involved visiting ships in the harbour, the Bethel had its own boats and, as the extract (right) from Lake's 1913 *Almanac* shows, there were three vessels in use at that time. In 1929 *Clareen* had been removed to London and *Three Sisters* was not adequate for work in the deep harbour and bay. Mrs Davey presented the motor boat shown above in memory of her husband, Richard Davey. After 116 years of service in the port, the Bethel closed its doors in October 1936 because, as a pamphlet issued to commemorate the occasion expressed it, 'With the change that has come over the shipping life of the port and with the development of the ship-repairing industry, the shipping trade has been diverted to the Docks, and with the object of catering for the men who land at and depart from the Docks, the British Sailors' Society purchased Armyn House, Bar Road and converted it to a Sailor's Rest. The Society could not see its way to carry on the Bethel as well and that building will be closed.' It is pleasing to note that Armyn House is still in use by the British Sailors' Society.

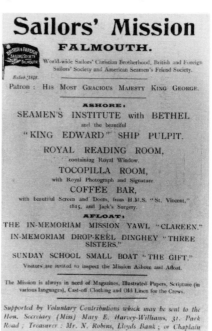

Sailors' Mission
FALMOUTH.

World-wide Sailors' Christian Brotherhood, British and Foreign Sailors' Society and American Seamen's Friend Society.

Estab. 1848.

Patron : His Most Gracious Majesty King George.

ASHORE:

SEAMEN'S INSTITUTE with BETHEL
and the beautiful
"KING EDWARD" SHIP PULPIT.

ROYAL READING ROOM,
containing Royal Window.

TOCOPILLA ROOM,
with Royal Photograph and Signature.

COFFEE BAR,
with beautiful Screen and Doors, from H.M.S. "St. Vincent," 1815, and Jack's Surgery.

AFLOAT:

THE IN-MEMORIAM MISSION YAWL "CLAREEN."

IN-MEMORIAM DROP-KEEL DINGHEY "THREE SISTERS."

SUNDAY SCHOOL SMALL BOAT "THE GIFT."

Visitors are invited to inspect the Mission Ashore and Afloat.

The Mission is always in need of Magazines, Illustrated Papers, Scripture (in various languages), Cast-off Clothing and Old Linen for the Crews.

Supported by Voluntary Contributions which may be sent to the Hon. Secretary (Miss) Mary E. Harvey-Williams, 31, Park Road ; Treasurer : Mr. N. Robins, Lloyds Bank ; or Chaplain J. C. Badger, Sailors' Mission, Falmouth.

This picture of the outer arm of Custom House Quay basin shows how narrow it was before the widening in 1903, the year that all the piers along the waterfront were improved. On the far side is a quay punt sailing into the quay, the Submarine Pier, the sheds of Fox Stanton timber merchants on the Bar, and the tall Falmouth Hotel prior to its western end extension in 1898.

Three vessels of the Penzance fishing fleet in the north-east corner of North Quay with a trading ketch and a topsail schooner, while on the quay on the far side a horse and cart is being loaded, probably with coal from the schooner. The large Quay House behind these sailing vessels was for many years the headquarters of the merchant supplying coal to steam ships, but this picture is probably the office and works of Fred L. Earle, printer.

Compared with earlier views of the Custom House Quay basin, this shows several notable changes. Taken in the early 1950s, the eighteen boats of the St Ives pilchard fleet are motorized with no vestige of sails except for a mizzen on the mast at the stern which is used to steady the vessel when in motion and reduce rolling. On the extreme right lie some of the motor-driven quay punts while, on the outside of the basin, the air-sea rescue launches, based in the port to work in conjunction with the helicopters of the Royal Naval Air Station at Culdrose, are anchored. There are two floating docks alongside the Empire and King's Wharves. The flat roof in the foreground began its life as an air-raid shelter during the war but was adapted after 1945 for leisure purposes when the wall on the far side had been removed. In those days the Quay basin was used regularly for swimming and children changed in the shelter; the Falmouth Swimming Club held its competitions here and water polo was played regularly until the water was declared unfit because of pollution.

Over the years Falmouth has been the destination of many sailors crossing the Atlantic in many different kinds of craft. The first small motorized boat may be seen after its crossing on p. 40, and in 1938 an American, Dwight Long, achieved one of the first single-handed journeys in his yacht *Idle Hour*. This picture shows a most unusual vessel tied up along-side the southern arm of Custom House Quay. After the crossing of the Pacific Ocean by the balsa raft *Kon Tiki* in 1948, these two French-Canadians sailed the Atlantic on this raft, *L'Egare*, arriving in August 1956 to a thorough search by officers of HM Customs and Excise after the raft had been towed into harbour by the combined efforts of the lifeboats from the Lizard (*Duke of York*) and Falmouth (*Crawford and Constance Conybeare*). In one of the most widely publicized voyages, in August 1965, Robert Manry sailed over in his 13 ft 6 in yacht *Tinkerbelle*, having been accompanied from the Lizard by a large flotilla of boats containing the inevitable reporters and TV cameramen which all such crossings seem to attract. On shore there was a civic welcome from the mayor, Mr Sam Hooper, accompanied by Manry's wife and children. The St Stythians band played 'The Star-Spangled Banner' but their efforts were drowned by the cheering of the large crowd. Just recently, arrivals have become more frequent with boats getting smaller and smaller, and crossings even made in a bottle-shaped boat. Where will it all end?

Falmouth has been a lifeboat station since 1867 when the *City of Gloucester* was delivered to the town by the Great Western Railway. The port supported a succession of rowing lifeboats until *The Brothers*, a motor lifeboat, arrived in 1931. In the first year of the Second World War the best-loved boat ever to have served in Falmouth, the *Crawford and Constance Conybeare*, costing £9,500, was accepted as a gift from the Conybeare family on 13 January 1940. Only five days later her first, most hazardous service took place when SS *Kirkpool* went aground on the rocks at Castle Beach: thirty-five men were resuced and Coxswain Snell received the Institution's Silver Medal. Above: the lifeboat posing in the Quay basin in 1956 with her crew, left to right, Len West, Arthur 'Toby' West, Wally Brown, Willy Arthur, Bert West, Barry Jago, Barry Timmins and Doug Gregory. Below: the annual lifeboat church service at the Quay is in progress in 1960 with one of the boat's most loyal supporters, Ken Williams, in the bow, the congregation seated on North Quay and the fitting background of large ships in Falmouth Docks.

That part of the Inner Harbour which lies off the town's main street has been an anchorage for a wide variety of ships over the years. In the heyday of the Packet Service, they lay here at anchor, in what was then known as the King's Road, awaiting the mail from London before sailing to one of the many destinations in Iberia, the Mediterranean or across the Atlantic. The photograph above, taken soon after 1930, shows the unmistakable *Cutty Sark* with the fishery protection vessel *Dart* and Lord St Leven's launch *Lady Bee* inshore of her while, to the right, the general purpose vessel *Restorer* has two tugs, *Northgate Scot* and *Victor*, on her inshore side. The white yacht in the centre is the 15 m yawl *Octavia* and the bow on the extreme right is that of the tug *Norgrove*. The post-war picture below is dominated by the Docks crane *Titania* (p. 74) and other utilitarian vessels from the dockyard such as a smaller crane, used mostly for mud-dredging, two craft fitted with staging for painting the sides of ships, a water barge, the oil barge *Witonia*, the ocean salvage tug *Masterman* and, steaming up river, a Dutch naval vessel probably on its way to tie up at the Caldy buoy on the extreme left.

This unusual aerial view can be dated to 1937. Apart from showing buildings long since demolished, such as Smithick School, the Grand Theatre and the Baptist church and Sunday School, the waterfront between the former gasworks (with collier alongside) and Prince of Wales' Pier shows up clearly. It illustrates well the narrowness of the main street and, just north of Fish Strand quay, the network of steel supports that once supported a wooden platform on which fishermen's nets were dried and on which stood the Fishermen's Rest.

Upton Slip is one of the few remaining 'opes' leading to the waterfront from the main street and the high ground to the west. Named after Captain Upton, who was mayor in 1708, it is a continuation seaward of Well Lane, the scene of cholera epidemics as recently as 1852 and of gastro-enteritis in 1899. Many of the town's working men have gone to their employment down this steep, uneven alley and several tradesmen lived here. These two figureheads stand at its lower end; the large one on the left is something of a mystery but that above it came from the schooner *Volante*, broken up at Little Falmouth in 1918.

The steep entrance to Fish Strand quay, built about 1790 and extended in 1871, is now best known as the somewhat hazardous way out of the Church Street car park but it used to be part of a working waterfront. The 1827 *Directory*, published by J. Philp whose workshop was situated there, records a ships' chandler and coal merchant, a spirit dealer, a saddler and trunk maker, a boot and shoe maker and a chemist and druggist. By 1842 the businesses had changed somewhat and included a bookseller, bookbinder, stationer and musical instrument seller, a black and white smith, a boot and shoe maker, a carpenter and joiner, a builder and stonemason, a fruiterer, a saddler and harness maker and a sailmaker. Later records locate the Crown and Anchor Inn at the top and Chard's Iceworks near the bottom of the narrow quay which derives its name from the Fish Market which was at one time at the top of the hill at No. 1 Church Street. As early as 1849 the *West Briton* had reported that the Borough Council had banned the display of fish in the market upon penalty of £5 on account of a cholera outbreak and that the poor fishermen had to hawk their fish about and sell it at half price 'doing it with a stealthiness more becoming hawkers of stolen property than persons honestly employed'.

The distinctive bow windows of the King's Arms Hotel on the extreme right show that this is the inland end of the Market Strand Pier built in 1871. The glass-fronted shops and the toll-booth further left were built after the pier. The crop of notice boards on the outside of the booth give details of loading charges and local bye-laws relating to the pier, as well as the charges to which the watermen were entitled, such as 4d. to Flushing, 3d. to Fish Strand or Custom House Quays and 1s. 6d. to Penryn, ending with 'No boatman may refuse a fare without reasonable grounds for doing so and the hirer shall be at liberty to prevent any other person from being a passenger with him.'

The outer end of Market Strand pier in the 1890s, with *Queen of the Fal* (left), Benney and Co.'s largest steamer, and *Roseland* of the St Mawes Steam Tug and Passenger Co. Ltd. *Queen of the Fal* was sold to London tug owners in 1911 and replaced by a larger vessel of the same name a year later, but *Roseland* qualifies as the longest serving passenger boat in the port. On the extreme right are some of the boats used to carry passengers and goods to vessels anchored out in the harbour.

In July 1903 the Duke and Duchess of Cornwall, later to become King George V and Queen Mary, came to stay with Lord and Lady Falmouth at Tregothnan for the ceremony of Benediction of the Nave of Truro Cathedral. While in the county the royal couple came to Falmouth by boat to lay the foundation stone of the Prince of Wales' Pier (see *Falmouth* p. 114). In the picture above the ceremony is in progress, with the Duke, in top hat, behind the stone, the distinctive figure of the Duchess with the parasol, and a vigilant crane operator on the extreme right carefully controlling the lowering of the stone (which was later moved to its present position on the pier). Lined up alongside the old pier in the lower picture are four boats and sailors from the naval sailing brigs out in the harbour, top left. Many spectator boats lie off both sides of the old pier, some of them seemingly dangerously overloaded. The eventual length of the new pier has been laid out with staging at the end of the old stone pier and the two separate structures are still to be seen clearly.

Built of steel in Carrickfergus in 1892, *Mary B. Mitchell* was used for coastal trading by successive owners until bought by Baron Penrhyn in 1912 as a cruiser. Commandeered during 1916 she was converted to a decoy or 'Q' ship in Falmouth and armed with several large guns. After two years' sailing in the waters of the south-west, tempting German submarines to surface, during which time several of her crew were decorated, she was opened to the public as she lay alongside Prince of Wales' Pier (above) to raise money for War Bonds (see *Falmouth* p. 139). After the war she was sold to James Tyrell of Arklow and returned to the far less exciting task of coastal trading, and below she is tied up alongside Falmouth gasworks, unloading coal. In 1923 she was converted to a twin-screw motor schooner and used mainly in the china clay trade between Par and Runcorn. Her end came in 1944 when, after sailing from Dublin with a crew of seven, she ran before a strong westerly gale and went aground in the Solway Firth; the crew was rescued by the Solway lifeboat but *Mary B. Mitchell* became a total loss.

In July 1905 a larger twin-screw steamer *Deerhound* replaced *Lady of the Isles*, damaged off Lamorna Cove on the route to the Isles of Scilly, and, as the *West Briton* somewhat optimistically announced, 'the discomforts which attend those who are not good sailors . . . will be considerably minimized'. *Deerhound* was 190 ft long and carried 437 passengers at 16 knots, was lit by electricity, had three decks, two large saloons and a promenade deck extending the entire length of the boat. Her maiden voyage was arranged by the directors for 320 shareholders and friends on a three hour trip to the Lizard. In addition to her scheduled voyages, other trips were organized along the coast and here, in 1906, *Deerhound* is seen alongside Prince of Wales' Pier on one of these excursions from Penzance, awaiting the return of her passengers. Passenger-tug *Victor*, with the Maltese cross on the funnel, lies on the opposite side of the pier.

On the north side of Smithick Creek in the seventeenth century an area known as Mulberry Square developed where many of the town's early merchants lived. By the end of the nineteenth century it was an area of crowded tenements with more than thirty inhabitants, but early in this century it was cleared to become the yard of the Falmouth Coal Supply Company. Here, the Padstow schooner *Iona* is unloading using the precarious technique described on p. 95. The board on the facing wall reads: 'Falmouth Coal Supply Company – Best South Wales, Northumberland and Lancashire Steam and House Coal – Coke and Firewood – Shipping and Yachts Supplied – Orders received within.'

The stretch of waterfront north of the Prince of Wales' Pier in the inter-war years was still a working area with shipyards and associated activities. Running seaward from the parallel High Street were several areas of working class housing – Seaview Cottages (all that survives), Briton's Yard (or Peterhouse or Queen's Court), Jane's Yard, Barracks Ope and Geach's Cottages. The tall windowed building on the quay right of centre is the Greenbank Laundry, on either side of which was a boatyard: on the nearside was Jackett's Victoria Yard, and on the far side Gray's Well Yard. The Jackett yard, figured below in the 1913 Lake's *Almanac*, built and maintained many of the boats of members of the nearby Royal Cornwall Yacht Club, including H.S. Tuke, the local artist, who was a keen sailor. This quay, known to many locals as Laundry Quay, has been renamed 'Admiral's Quay' for development purposes.

The Greenbank Hotel is the turning point for this rather grand parade, but of most interest here are the sheds and workshops on the seaward (left) side in what is now Greenbank Gardens. This was once the headquarters of Olver and Sons, founded in 1811. In addition to building St Anthony Lighthouse and erecting Black Rock beacon they built Falmouth's new Town Hall on the Moor in 1864, all the railway stations on the line between Truro and Falmouth, the Falmouth Union Workhouse (1851), and many of the houses along Dunstanville Terrace, Harbour Terrace, Harriet Place, Stratton Terrace and Tehidy Terrace. In their role of undertakers, they were responsible in May 1875 for embalming the bodies of victims of the wreck of the *Schiller* on the Isles of Scilly, whose relatives wished them to be returned to the USA. But, as the older partners retired, the younger members of the family did not wish to carry on so the business ceased to exist. The workshops were taken over by Spear Bros, a coachbuilding firm (above), but in 1913 the Borough Council converted the whole area into the Greenbank Gardens.

The Royal Cornwall Yacht Club was formed in 1872 and its clubhouse for the first ten years of its existence was the Greenbank Hotel. In 1883 Greenbank House was leased from its owner, Miss Glasson, and in 1911 the building was purchased by a syndicate of the Club members. Many alterations had to be carried out as the land in front of the building had been used as a coal store; several structures had to be removed to give the superb view of the harbour which can now be enjoyed from the lawn in front of the club. This picture shows the arrangement in 1908.

This comprehensive view of the whole Greenbank area shows the relative positions of several features already mentioned: from Well Beach on the extreme left, the Royal Cornwall Yacht Club, the former workshops of Olver and Sons, and the Greenbank Hotel and quay. In January 1835 a report was published by Henry Habberly Price, Civil Engineer, for the improvement of this stretch of water, referred to as 'the anchorage for His Majesty's Packets', the introduction to which gives his reason: 'Having been requested by . . . Lord de Dunstanville and Lord Wodehouse (the principal lords of the soil of Falmouth and its vicinity) to survey and examine the Packet anchorage . . . formerly called the King's Road, to ascertain its present state with the practicability of deepening same and to estimate the cost . . . for the purpose of giving such additional depth and accommodation, as the superior class of vessels . . . to be employed in his Majesty's Packet Service on this station appear to require.' Eventually, the packet ships were removed from Falmouth and the remarkably detailed report forgotten. The opulent houses along Dunstanville Terrace and Stratton Place run across the picture as far as the Greenbank Hotel, their steep back gardens stretching up the hillside to Penwerris (formerly, Middle) Terrace. This whole area was in Budock parish up to 1892 when Falmouth Borough was enlarged to include the developing suburbs of Penwerris. The narrow main street has led to many suggestions over the years that a harbourside road, promenade or esplanade should be built along part or the whole of the waterfront to relieve congestion. As early as 1827, when the street was much narrower than it is today, Richard Thomas wrote in his *History of the Town and Harbour of Falmouth*, 'The town might be greatly improved by constructing an esplanade or terrace (which has been often talked of) extending along the whole of its front from Greenbank to the Pier, and out nearly to low water mark, there being ample room for such a work and the expense would be repaid by letting the inner part of the ground thus gained for a line of buildings to front the harbour; besides which carriages might then avoid the present narrow way through High Street.' In July 1893, soon after the enlargement of the borough, plans were prepared for an esplanade between Market Strand pier and Dunstanville Terrace between forty and fifty-seven feet wide, and again in October 1929, when 'the cost of such a promenade from Greenbank to Grove Place was reckoned as £400,000'. 'Mr G. Stock proposed a road 120 ft wide with junctions to present streets; twelve acres of land would be reclaimed and it would solve the traffic problems for years to come. It would attract large hotels, boarding houses and shopping arcades, offering about 150 frontages at £100 per annum with a 99-year lease; it would also absorb the unemployed.' Mr J. Harris described it as 'a mad-brained scheme' which would bankrupt the town and rates would have to rise by six shillings in the pound. The Chamber of Commerce was also against it, stressing that many businesses would have to be compensated and suggested, instead, a new road between Gyllyngvase and Swanpool. To this day, the subject is still being discussed but the cost has made its realization highly improbable; instead, pedestrianization seems to be the preferred option.

Some time in the sixteenth century a Penryn merchant named Boyer built cellars, probably for processing pilchards for export, in the outer part of 'the manor of Penryn Forryn', no doubt because the water was deeper there and the site was nearer to the open sea than at the Penryn quays. Ever since then the location has been known as Boyer's Cellars, although it has at times been referred to as 'Liverpool Wharf', and 'Coast Lines', when the wharves in that area were used by vessels of a shipping company with that name. Originally, coastal traffic was operated by a large number of small, usually family firms using, firstly, schooners and ketches and, later, steamers to carry goods between coastal locations because it was easier and cheaper than the comparatively poor land communications. In 1917 three such small firms combined to form 'Coast Lines' and, based on Liverpool, traded to London, across the Irish Sea and into the Bristol Channel, carrying general cargo, live cattle and passengers. Falmouth was one of their several ports of call and their steamers each with a black funnel with a white 'V' and names ending in 'Coast', became regular and familiar visitors to the harbour. At first cargoes were landed in the Docks, but later goods were discharged over the side into steam barges (as shown above) in the inner harbour for destinations in Falmouth, Penryn and Truro. In February 1928 the *Penryn Advertiser* reported that the company applied for a reduction in dues on these barges of 25s. per vessel as only a small amount of cargo was handled and the company was likely to use road transport from the Falmouth depot at Boyer's Cellars, which it eventually did. In 1936 Coast Lines bought the foreshore at the Cellars from the Mead family, dredged the creek at that point and installed unloading facilities so that, from 1938 onwards, the coasters could come alongside. During the Second World War many of their vessels were commandeered and involved in operations in Norway, Normandy, Italy, Greece and North Africa, and several were sunk. Business peaked in the 1950s despite considerable competition from road transport, and in 1958 the company owned 110 ships, carried half a million cattle and over a million passengers on their ten-day cruises between Liverpool and London. But, eventually, container traffic and large lorries proved more convenient and cheaper for their customers and there was a gradual decline until 1970 when the business was taken over by P&O and coastal operations ceased.

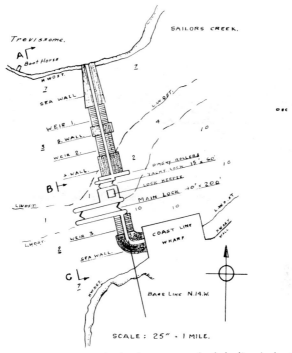

Although Penryn owes its existence to its harbour, a gradual decline in its trade after the mid-seventeenth century was due largely to the silting up of its river together with the growth of its new neighbour on deeper water nearer the open sea. Yet there was a distinct revival of business between about 1850 and 1939 as a result of the granite, coal and cattle trade. Several plans have been suggested for a bridge over the river below the Borough, such as the Flushing Road and Pier Bill promoted by Lord Clinton of Trefusis in 1813 which was dropped after opposition from Penryn. Even more far-reaching plans were put forward in July 1845, such as that shown above, in the Falmouth Docks (Penryn Creek) Act for the purpose of 'deepening, regulating and otherwise improving Falmouth harbour . . . and for forming basins, docks and other works in Penryn Creek . . . and for penning up the waters in the said creek . . . and to construct an embankment at or near the entrance to the creek'. It included a dredged channel out into Carrick Roads, a road across the embankment 'for passengers, animals, carts and carriages', an exemption from tolls for vessels less than 150 tons conveying goods to and from Penryn, as well as 'steam towing vessels', and allowed the occupier of Boyer's Cellars to ship 2,000 tons of cargo annually free of rates and duties with the same concession to Lord Clinton and on any goods from Trefusis and all agricultural produce from Flushing to Falmouth. But by the time all this was sorted out the increase in the size of ships, especially the new steam vessels, had rendered the plans obsolete, and the new Falmouth Docks Act of 1859 changed the location to where it may be seen today. In 1859–60 Lord Clinton planned to extend Flushing eastwards and build a new town on Trefusis Point; a swing bridge between Greenbank and Flushing was also proposed but neither scheme ever got off the drawing board. In 1891 the Falmouth, Penryn and Flushing Bridge, Dam and Tidal Basin Bill was proposed, which included a swing bridge at Boyer's Cellars, but the mayor of Penryn said it was 'detrimental to Penryn's interests and ruinous to the trade of the port' and that too was withdrawn.

Round the corner from Boyer's Cellars is the small, tidal Turnpike Creek, which takes its name from the toll-gate which once stood at its landward end. Known as the 'Falmouth gate', it controlled both roads into the town from Penryn: the first, called Penryn Old Road on Thomas's 1827 map (now known as Old Hill), and the second, Penryn New Road on the Thomas map, built about 1800 past Boyer's Cellars and Greenbank to the top of High Street. The toll-house, shown above, was carefully preserved by the original builders of the garage as part of the town's heritage but, regrettably, demolished by the next owners. The creek itself was a location for the building and laying-up of boats, especially after the takeover of the Bar area by the Docks in the mid-1920s, but the saddest sight of all used to be the rotting timbers of many grand old sailing vessels left there to disintegrate (below) as steam vessels took over the coastal trade.

During the last century drastic changes have taken place at Ponsharden creek, pictured here in the early 1930s. In 1867, Penryn Corporation took over much of the hitherto unused foreshore and 'fundus' (the sea floor) including Ponsharden (in those days often referred to as 'Poundsharden'), and 'a parcel of the Manor of Penryn Forryn' was let to Francis John Holm on which he erected a boathouse. In November, 1872, as part of the 'Penryn and Helston Railway and Tramway Bill' for which support was being sought in a notice in the *Penryn Advertiser*, Ponsharden was scheduled to have a railway when a line was proposed from Penryn station to a point near the creek, from where a tramway would run along the turnpike road back into the lower part of the town, crossing the bridge and ending near the junction of Commercial Road and New Street. Like so many such plans, this one failed for want of financial support. In July 1878, tenders were requested for the use of the creek to be sent to the Town Council for an annual tenancy and it is likely that Emanuel Martin established a boatyard there: during the 1880s he built the ketches *Irene* and *Leader* and the fishing smack *Daisy* for use in the North Sea. But in September 1891, the *Penryn Advertiser* reported that Martin, referred to as 'a Budock shipbuilder' – the creek was then in Budock Parish – had gone bankrupt. After that the yard was probably taken over by 'one of Falmouth's best known shipbuilders', shipwright W.J. Burt, several generations of whose family have been until recently involved in boat building and repairing in Falmouth. He had served his apprenticeship at his father's yard at the Bar and helped to build the quay punt ICU (p. 94) but he was not a good businessman and the yard was soon in the hands of the Exe Transport Company, for whom Burt worked, followed by Capt. W.H. Dowman who lived on the opposite shore of the Penryn river at Trevisome House. W.J. Burt carried on working in the yard and carried out the re-rigging of the *Cutty Sark* when Capt. Dowman brought her to Falmouth in 1923. After a period of inactivity, except for the Second World War when fitting out and maintenance was done on fast coastal craft, the creek was used by the Dredge and Marine Company after the war who built the present King Harry Ferry in 1974.

Probably the largest vessels ever to be seen in the Penryn river at anchor off the entrance to Ponsharden creek; they represent a small part of the large fleet of redundant steamers laid up after the First World War in various creeks of the estuary awaiting either a return to service or, as was more likely, a trip to the breaker's yard. On the shore on the left is the road between Falmouth and Penryn which was widened in 1931. Beside the Falmouth road a number of coastal schooners lie alongside Glasson's Quay, long since buried under material dumped to reclaim land for factory and office building. In the distance Penryn rises up the hillside away from the river.

Fishing Boats, River Fal, Falmouth

The busy ship repair yard at Ponsharden probably in the 1920s, with Boyer's Cellars visible beyond the large vessels in the foreground. The misleading nature of some postcard captions is illustrated here all too clearly: none of the boats is likely to have been used for fishing, this is not the River Fal and the scene is in the Borough of Penryn! The varied boats shown include a topsail schooner and several private yachts either laid up or undergoing repair.

This close-up view of the Ponsharden dry dock shows a very unusual vessel undergoing repair. It is probably the only tug ever owned by the Royal National Lifeboat Institution and on the stern is written *Helen Peele: RNLI Padstow*. In harbours such as Falmouth there were always commercial tugs available to tow the rowing lifeboats to the scene of a disaster but this was not the case at Padstow, where the lifeboat not only had a long distance to travel to reach vessels in distress but had to traverse the aptly named Doom Bar at the seaward end of the Camel estuary. After a tragic disaster in 1897, when eight lifeboatmen were lost, the RNLI decided to station its own tug to assist the operations of the Padstow boats (the port was unique in having two lifeboats permanently stationed there). Built in Leith, 95 ft long with twin screws (visible in the picture), *Helen Peele* had a speed of 10 knots and was highly manoeuvrable. Named after the wife of a legatee, Charles J. Peele, the tug arrived in Padstow in September 1901 with a new lifeboat, *Edmund Harvey*, in tow and immediately experienced the hazards of the Camel estuary by going aground on the Doom Bar, the lifeboat assisting to refloat her. After that the two vessels worked together for twenty-eight years although the tug frequently operated alone to save abandoned vessels or to assist rescues at other lifeboat stations. When, in 1929, a motor lifeboat was stationed at Padstow, *Helen Peele* was sold as a yacht tender. The small dry dock shown here was in use until after the Second World War when it was filled in by one of the several companies to work at Ponsharden.

One of the most famous of the many ships built in the yards around the Fal estuary was *Lady of Avenel*, seen here rigged as a brigantine. Built at Trethowan's Little Falmouth yard as a schooner, she was launched in July 1874 for E.D. Anderton, a Falmouth merchant. She changed hands several times and after the First World War was fitted with an auxiliary engine. After a voyage to Spitzbergen she was bought by Captain W.H. Dowman who brought her back to Falmouth, fitted her out as a training ship for boys, and moored her in the Penryn river between Flushing and Greenbank (inset) until he bought the *Cutty Sark* for the same purpose in 1923. Renamed *Island*, she was fitted out in the Ponsharden yard for a voyage of exploration to the Arctic in 1925, and while in the yard was opened to the public in aid of the Mayor of Penryn's Disaster Fund (left). Laid up for several years on her return, she underwent several changes of ownership before returning to Cornwall in 1933, was fitted out as a yacht, rigged as a brigantine and made a number of coastal voyages which included the 1937 Spithead Review. After this varied and adventurous career she was finally abandoned in Poole harbour during the Second World War and was slowly rotting away when blown up in 1955.

Penryn and Flushing

This engraving of 'Penryn from Fish Cross', published by John Gill and Son, shows the most characteristic feature of the ancient borough, the Town Hall and Market House dividing the main street into Upper and Lower Market Street. John Gill came to Penryn in 1831 when he set up in business as a printer. In 1840 he was appointed Overseer of the Poor and joined the Quakers in 1849. But he became best known as publisher of the *Commercial, Shipping and General Advertiser* for West Cornwall in June 1867, which later became known as the *Penryn Advertiser*. For the next thirty years he recorded the notable events of the town, week by week, and this tradition was continued by Frederick Chegwidden who not only took over the business in 1898 but whose family looked after John Gill until he died in 1905 at the age of 94. His original shop is seen here, the third on the lower side of Market Street.

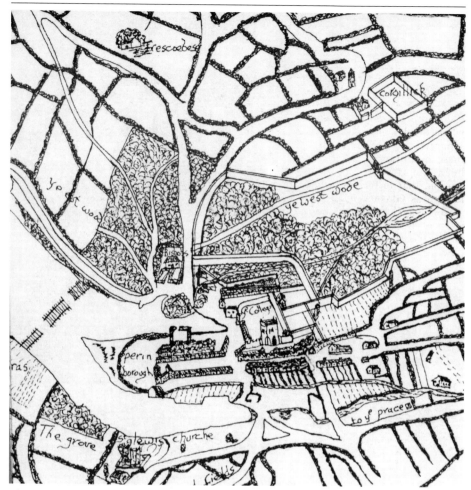

This extract from the Burghley Map is dated 1580 although it is likely to have been of an earlier date as it shows Glasney College which was a victim of Henry VIII's Dissolution of the Monasteries between 1536 and 1539. Penryn owes its existence to the Charter of Enfranchisement by Bishop Brewer in 1236 and the foundation of the religious educational establishment in 1265. The College became known all over the Christian world as a centre of learning but lawlessness was allowed to creep in: because of its popularity the clergy tended to stay too long and their behaviour, as well as that of the townsfolk, left much to be desired. A port developed on its waterside site and smuggling became rife. To defend itself against attack from the sea, despite its inland location, not only was the College turned into a military stronghold in the 1530s (Leland described it as 'strongly walled and encastled having three strong towers and guns at the but of the creek') but, to discourage seaborne attack, a row of palisades was built across the river below the town, as shown above, with the gaps obstructed with chains should an emergency arise. The map shows the extensive woodland in which the townsfolk were often caught poaching the deer, as well as the location of Trescobeas, transcribed from the Cornish as the 'Bishop's Dwelling Without'.

The defensive nature of Glasney College, with its high, castellated walls and guard towers on each side of the main gate, is shown clearly on this extract from the 'Great Map of the West'. Known originally as Parc Hellan the town grew up on the peninsula, which divides the river into two separate creeks. The names of these two branches has always been a matter of some contention, that in the south being known as Glasney, College or Budock Creek, while the northern waterway has been called the St Gluvias Creek or Manamor. The road southwards to Arwenack and Pendennis crosses a bridge at the head of the Glasney Creek, at the bottom of the present St Thomas's Street.

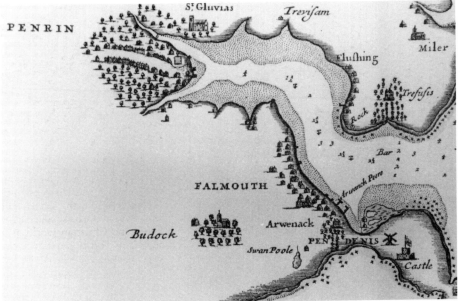

This section of the excellent sea chart published by Greenvile Collins in 1693 shows the relative positions of Penryn and its younger, downstream neighbours, Falmouth and Flushing. Glasney has no place on this map despite the fact that as late as 1739 Tonkin wrote that one watch tower and part of the wall were still standing. At about this time the population of Penryn was between 900 and 1,000 people, about the same as Truro which was already one of the county's main towns.

This 1816 engraving shows the essentially waterside nature of the town in the early nineteenth century. A fair (1259) and market (1311) had been granted early in the town's existence and Penryn had legally become a port when a portreeve was appointed to oversee the sale of goods and cattle. After Glasney had ceased to exist, the piracy, smuggling and wrecking of the inhabitants had increased to such an extent that when, eighty years later, in 1621, James I granted a Royal Charter to 'the Maritime and Ancient populous Borough . . . occupying and exercising a market and having much traffic in and upon the sea . . . by reason of the exportation and importation of goods and merchandizes', it was noted 'the aforesaid borough through indolence for a long time . . . in the arrival of sailors and other unruly men resorting together divers riots and routs, also very many great offences are there often committed and perpetrated'. The townsfolk asked for a mayor and Corporation to administer the law of the land so that, as the Charter goes on, 'the borough hereafter shall remain a borough of peace and quietness to the dread and terror of evildoers', but the lawlessness continued, despite the fact that the first mayor, Sampson Bloye, was supported by two constables and allowed to build a prison. As so much smuggling was going on an Act was made in 1663 'for preventing frauds and regulating abuses'. A commission was set up to inspect the ports of Penryn, Truro and Falmouth and to establish sole landing places on behalf of the Exchequer in 1676, resulting in a quay being built at the eastern end of the port at the junction of the creeks (shown above) and this is still known as Exchequer Quay. It also attracted many Falmouth merchants who would not use the quay built by Sir Peter Killigrew in the 1670s.

Penryn's eighteenth-century trade was extremely varied, the records suggesting that such commodities as salt, timber, wine, tobacco, fish, pewter, tin, cloth and furniture were among the goods handled at Exchequer Quay. But with the arrival of the nineteenth century, much of the trade passed into the hands of large merchants dealing with special cargoes. In this picture *Hebe* lies alongside the quay, where dressed granite blocks await shipment, and behind the schooner the Custom House may be seen through the rigging, and the chimney and tall building of Mead's Paper Mill are to the right of the foremast. Owned by Bisson and Dawe, this vessel was probably one of several engaged in the cattle trade with Corunna in Spain. Other merchants in the business were Mead and Mitchell and J.B. Gray. Cattle were off-loaded, often by making them swim ashore to remove pests from their skins, at both Penryn and Falmouth, where there are records of sales of cattle in Carne's Rope Walk and on the Moor (see p. 130). Another lucrative traffic, in which smaller, faster vessels were engaged, was the fruit trade with the Azores and Mediterranean countries: rarely bigger than 150 tons, these ships were loaded carefully and quickly, with the cargo regularly inspected during the voyage. The merchants engaged in this trade were William Glasson, who built a quay which bore his name on the north side of Ponsharden creek, and Edwin Pope. The fruit trade in the second half of the last century was mostly based on large ports with an extensive hinterland, such as Bristol and London, but these two merchants brought many cargoes to Penryn and Falmouth. Others who helped make nineteenth-century Penryn a thriving port and industrial centre were the Freeman family, with granite (pp. 138–43), the West of England Bone and Manure Company, with guano and animal bones (p. 135), the Mead family, with milling and paper, and G.C. Fox and Co., with timber and general merchandise. In August 1869 the *West Briton* reported, 'Perhaps no town of its size in the Western Counties has been so flourishing during the past year as Penryn. Its ten steam engines have been constantly at work, employing a very large number of hands. The granite trade has been very brisk, the workmen earning from five to six shillings a day each, with full employment. The cattle trade has been steady throughout the year, upward of 2,500 cattle having been imported by two merchants whose ships have been constantly plying between France, Spain and Penryn. The iron foundry established in the town a few years ago has been constantly at work, employing a great number of hands under the spirited and able management of Mr Sara. The paper mills of Mr Mead are also doing a large amount of business and giving great employment. The potato trade has not flourished as in former years, owing no doubt to the excellence of the crops in England. In 1867 some cargoes of oranges were imported but none last year: it is said that the speculation did not pay. The owners of orchards and gardens, with which the neighbourhood abounds, find a ready sale for their produce from the great number of vessels constantly arriving at Falmouth. Tanyards, coal stores, lime kilns and flour mills also place the town commercially in a very healthy state.'

Timber and granite awaiting shipment or collection from a surprisingly empty quay. There were frequent complaints from carriers about delays caused by such obstructions on the quay, and in October 1903, when a cargo of stone for the roads landed in February from the St Keverne quarries had not been removed, complaints to the Council led to its immediate removal.

The annual Penryn Regatta attracted a large crowd to the Exchequer Quay to watch the sailing and rowing races and this 1913 picture shows some young spectators perilously perched on the hand-operated crane. This interesting photograph was donated by the late Mr P.J. Bearham who was the occupant of the pram on the extreme left. His mother's hand is resting on the pram handle and his bowler-hatted father is standing next to Paniggia's ice-cream cart.

The ketch *Penryn*, built at Rapson's yard about a hundred yards away on the other side of the creek below St Gluvias churchyard (seen in the picture below), lies alongside the quay. It is possible that the piles of roadstone on the quay could have been unloaded from the ketch. In the Second World War *Penryn* was adapted and fitted out as a hulk for the operation of one of the barrage balloons protecting Falmouth harbour against air attack.

The small steamer *Multistone* in the identical position, in the process of unloading a similar cargo. Loaded vessels such as this could only reach the quay at high tide and would rest on the mud as the tide fell. A similar type of ship would have been used to carry coal to Annear's yard adjacent to the quay, but it would unload directly into the coal yard. In August 1930 the *Penryn Advertiser* reported that SS *Belvedere*, 1,026 tons, with coal for J.C. Annear, was the largest vessel ever to visit the port.

Taken from near the site of the long-derelict Rapson's boat yard, this high tide photograph of the entrance to St Gluvias creek shows several features of interest. Extreme left is a view of Exchequer Quay from an unusual angle, with a topsail schooner lying in the basin at the bottom of Quay Hill. Over the years, this quay had been used to export many different commodities: in the late seventeenth century tin was an important export, especially after a blowing house had been established in the town in 1669; vessels from the port participated regularly in the Newfoundland fishery and the catch, together with pilchards from local waters, was taken to Mediterranean countries; timber for local sawmills was imported and granite exported; some china clay was carried out of the port in the 1870s from a pit opened at St Day. The four black roofs to the right of the quay are the Cattle Lairs, where animals imported from Spain were kept before sale or slaughter. To their right a row of stone buildings stretches off to the head of the creek, most of them occupied by the businesses with a frontage on Commercial Road. Behind the Lairs, the tall building with a chimney is Mead's Paper Mill which had been producing paper as early as 1791 under William Tucker and Richard Rowe at what was then the Lower Tresooth Mill. In 1821 the *West Briton* reported that the premises had been fitted up for an oil or mustard mill, but soon after this the brothers James, Joseph and John Mead occupied them as a flour and paper mill. Not long afterwards flour milling ceased on this site, and after steam machinery was installed in 1844 several types of paper were manufactured such as 'printing, cartridge, brown wrapping, butter papers, caps and small hands'. The mill had its own small quay near the works on the shore of this creek. Lake's *Parochial History* of 1868 emphasized the manufacture of straw paper, 'large quantities of which are sent weekly to London: the oaten straw is collected from farms within a twenty mile radius'. Rags were also used and these were gathered from the surrounding area by a team of women. Fires were frequent at this mill, the earliest in 1860 when Meads were using part of it as a corn store. Later, in September 1880, when the second storey was found to be ablaze, the *Falmouth News Slip* reported, 'The Penryn engine was quickly on the spot but the want of proper appliances and organization rendered them of little value and great confusion prevailed.' The Falmouth brigade arrived three-quarters of an hour after bugle call and their efforts were directed to keeping the fire from spreading; on its way to Penryn, the Falmouth brigade encountered dense fog and were doubtful as to the whereabouts of the fire. Property worth £30,000 was destroyed. Fifteen years later, flames were seen coming through the roof. The fire was confined to the main building, and although a small block containing valuable stocks of paper was saved great damage was done to valuable machinery.

Further up St Gluvias creek were more industries with private quays as well as the rear of private houses on Commercial Road which ran parallel to the creek. Many of these suffered from floods at high spring tides especially when they coincided with an easterly gale. In February 1885, for instance, a 3 ft wave swept up the river and flooded the whole of waterside Penryn. Ground floors in Commercial Road had eighteen inches of water; Rickard's stores lost £70 worth of flour, cement, manure and machinery while bark floated out of J.F. Reed's tannery and extensive damage was done to the moulding shop of the Sara and Burgess foundry. Boats were rowed along Commercial Road rescuing the pigs which nearly all residents kept in their yards.

The Custom House on Exchequer Quay forms the background to the large group of people attracted by the photographer. Behind it are the sheds of the Freeman granite yard. The chimney to the right is in the timber yard of Fox Stanton, while in the centre is the swing bridge taking the road across the Budock Creek to Falmouth. In the background rise the fields of Eastwood Farm.

BOROUGH OF PENRYN.

Cattle Plague

ORDERS.

NOTICE IS HEREBY GIVEN that the Lords of Her Majesty's Privy Council have by an Order dated the 11th day of October, 1867, defined the part of the BOROUGH OF PENRYN, within which FOREIGN CATTLE may be landed, as follows :—

All that space in the town of Penryn lying between the south-western side of the Commercial road and the Penryn River, from the Budock Creek to the northern end of Gluvias-street ; also the space occupied by the lairs in the occupation of Mr. John Gray, and the lairs and slaughter-house in the occupation of Mr. Dawe, adjoining Commercial-road on the south-western side of that road, between Budock Creek and Gluvias-street, which spaces are coloured pink on the plan of part of the town of Penryn, deposited at the Privy Council Office, a copy of which is deposited at the Office of the Town Clerk of the Borough of Falmouth; and do prescribe as follows :—

1. All foreign cattle landed within the said defined part of the port shall be slaughtered within four days after the landing thereof, exclusive of the day of landing, unless they are taken to a licensed market or sale within that defined part within such four days, and they shall be so taken if a market or sale is held there within the said period of four days but if there is no such licensed market or sale within that defined part, or if no such market or sale is held there within the said period of four days, then all such foreign cattle shall be slaughtered within that defined part within the said period of four days.

2. Cattle other than foreign cattle within the said defined part shall not be removed therefrom alive.

AND NOTICE IS HEREBY ALSO GIVEN that a Copy of the plan above referred to, is also deposited at the office of the Town Clerk of the said Borough of Penryn

(BY ORDER.)

Geo. A. Jenkins.

Town Clerk of the Borough of Penryn.

Dated Town Clerk's Office, Penryn, November 7th, 1867.

This extract from the *Penryn Advertiser* of 7 November 1867 illustrates one of the hazards of the cattle-importing business, an important part of Penryn's trade in the second half of the nineteenth century, encouraged by the growing demands of the Cornish mining community. Fast schooners carried, on average, between forty and sixty cattle in specially adapted holds with special arrangements made for water supply for the animals. Early imports were landed at Falmouth, brought ashore at the Market Strand and sold at a market on the Moor, but later most cargoes went to Penryn. The epidemic of rinderpest was met with strict precautions, and by the later months of 1867 the measures described here seem to have eradicated the disease. At first, cattle were landed at private quays or on Exchequer Quay or were made to swim ashore downstream at Ponsharden at low tide. In 1881 Penryn Corporation decided to erect the Cattle Lairs 'for the more orderly import of cattle' at a cost of about £500. By 1883 over £1,200 had been earned by charging sixpence for each beast landed within the port limits. Local newspapers carried regular reports of the trade, and in September 1875 the *Falmouth Packet* announced: 'Additions are being rapidly made to the number of vessels employed in the importation of Spanish cattle to Penryn from Corunna. Messrs J. Gray and Sons are fitting out the *Stone*, a fine schooner, for the trade and she, it is said, will be followed by a vessel now owned by another firm. The *Emu*, Capt. Kent, belonging to Messrs Mead and Mitchell, the *Victoria*, Capt. Hooper, Messrs Dawe and Bisson and *J.B. Gray*, Capt. Rich, Messrs Gray and Sons, all arrived on Saturday with between two and three hundred head of splendid fat beasts, all fit for the market. *J.B. Gray* brought the greatest number – 104 – and has made a fine passage. The beasts are in first class condition and attracted a number of admirers on their landing on Saturday night.' Arrivals were regularly reported in the *Penryn Advertiser*. Disasters often happened: in November 1875 a storm in the Bay of Biscay caused extensive damage to *J.B. Gray* and two seamen were lost overboard; and in April 1881 the schooner *Flora*, bound for Penryn, ended up in Ilfracombe, driven off course by contrary winds after thirteen days at sea with sixty cattle on board for which water and fodder were almost exhausted.

A schooner and a steamer lie alongside the private quays in the St Gluvias creek. The buildings in the distance stand on what is today known as Islington Wharf. This was the location of one of Penryn's most famous industries, the foundry established by Nicholas Sara and John Burgess, former craftsmen from the Perran foundry who set up soon after 1851 on the site of the former workhouse in Church Road and in 1869, built a second foundry on land below St Gluvias church. In 1875 Mr Sara applied to build a quay at the head of the creek and he was granted a 75 year lease on this piece of foreshore at a ground rent of £2 per annum. Several of their high-quality marine engines were installed in the passenger-tugs built by Cox and Co. or Pool, Skinner and Williams on the Bar, and they built the first King Harry Ferry in 1889.

Low tide in the St Gluvias creek. Rafts of timber lie on the mud, supporting, in the foreground, a nesting swan. Imported timber was seasoned in this way for several years, allowing the sea water to wash out its sap before being used in one of the local boatyards or sawn in the Fox Stanton timber yard at the entrance to the Budock creek. To the left of this photograph a footpath leaves the road immediately below the church and follows the creekside all the way to Flushing, making it one of the loveliest walks in the district, especially at high tide.

The solid granite building above is one of the few to survive virtually intact from the nine-teenth-century Commercial Road. It is the headquarters of the Penryn Transport Company, established after the First World War when mechanized road transport began to replace horse-drawn vehicles. An early lorry is seen below complete with solid tyres and, written above the cab, 'Phone 31 Penryn'. Two of the former cattle importers, Philip Dawe and John Gray, were now potato merchants. They imported fruit as well, and the newspapers often reported unusual discoveries, such as tarantulas, in these cargoes. In October 1926 the *Penryn Advertiser* recounted that in the stores of John Gray and Sons in a specially heated ripening room 'found in a nest of leaves and grass in a bunch of bananas imported from Jamaica' was a small monkey which had travelled by sea, rail and road.

Commercial Road did not exist until the early years of the nineteenth century; before then, the gardens of the houses on the north side of the town's main street swept down the hill to the creek shore and were often rented out to market gardeners who supplied their produce to ships in Penryn and Falmouth. As trade expanded quays were established at the end of the gardens and a road developed parallel to the creek. With the gradual increase in road transport in the inter-war years the need for widening what had been a very narrow street became increasingly urgent until, in 1927, the former Mead's paper mill and the whole west side was demolished and the road improved (above). The *Penryn Advertiser* reported in November 1927 that work had begun on resurfacing the road with eight inches of doubly reinforced concrete at a cost of £2,800 (below). The old surface had been badly damaged over the years at spring tides as water had seeped through crevices in the buildings to cover the road with between two and three feet of water.

With the development of Commercial Road it became increasingly obvious that a new bridge was required lower down the Budock creek than the original crossing at the bottom of St Thomas's Street. In 1828 the Helston Turnpike Trust erected a cast-iron swing-bridge so that access could be maintained to the several quays alongside the creek. Complaints about this bridge increased towards the end of the century as its surface was being broken up by the increasing volume of traffic, especially the traction engines used by Freeman's granite business. In October 1908 a new bridge, illustrated above, was installed, 45 ft long and 12½ ft wide, with a roadway in Jarrah wood set in asphalt; despite a total weight of about 50 tons it moved through 90 degrees horizontally, operated by hand from the deck of the bridge. The picture below shows the bridge in its open position to allow a vessel into the creek, probably the Coast Lines steam barge *Pennar* which, with its companion *Harfat*, would carry goods from the coasters to unload here. They also took goods up to Truro, sometimes with the dumb-barge *Penhallow* in tow.

The Budock or Glasney creek had been the principal landing place of Penryn for centuries. The growth of trade and industry in the nineteenth century saw both banks used for a variety of businesses and, upstream, in the suburb known long after the disappearance of Glasney as College, several water mills were in operation, powered from a leat taken from the College river. Granite and timber yards developed on the south side of the creek, and evidence of the former may be seen in these pictures. Dominating both pictures is the three-storey building on the north side of the creek of the West of England Bone and Manure Company which, after 1820 when a revolution in animal husbandry led to a vast increase in turnip production, began to import animal bones and guano to supply fertilizer.

The volume of road traffic along Commercial Road and across the bridge was increased after 1927 when J.C. Annear, Coal Merchant, offered the Town Council a rent of £32 per annum for a 75 year lease on what had been Martin's and Collett's yards, on which he built the distinctive building seen here at a cost of nearly £3,000. For several years strong views were regularly expressed about the swing-bridge and local newspapers reported the differences of opinion with relish. The County Council, which would have had to pay a good deal of the cost, turned down plans for improvements and opponents expressed a variety of views: a narrow bridge was a safety valve and prevented accidents; the bridge had been wide enough for years so what need was there to change it; improvement would be for the sole benefit of Falmouth and the ruin of Penryn. The mayor of Penryn was reported to have said, in July 1925, that the bridge ought to be done away with altogether and the gulf filled in. Few vessels used the small quay on the inland side of the bridge but Mr C. Sara thought the mayor's suggestion 'ridiculous' as it meant that vessels would have to discharge on the seaward side of the bridge and cargoes would have to be carted to the warehouses and stores instead of having them discharged on the premises. Other ideas were expressed, one being that the bridge be used only for road traffic with a new bridge for foot passengers. The Lord Lieutenant of Cornwall did not endear himself to Penryn folk by referring to the Budock creek as 'that small corner of mud', but as time went on it became increasingly apparent that the swing-bridge shown here was totally inadequate, common sense prevailed, the County Council agreed to pay most of the cost, and the idea of a wider, fixed bridge gained in popularity.

In the early 1930s scenes such as that shown above were becoming increasingly frequent as Penryn to Falmouth buses, commercial vehicles – both horse-drawn and motorized – for Freeman's granite works, Annear's coal depot, and the Fox Stanton timber yard (the probable destination of the timber-laden cart crossing the bridge in the picture) as well as a growing volume of through-traffic to Truro and beyond made the narrow bridge a troublesome bottleneck. Eventually, in 1934, the building of a wider, fixed bridge began. Movement across the bridge continued during the construction (as shown below) after the buildings shown to the left of the bus had been demolished. The new bridge was opened in 1935 and today's volume of traffic must be far greater than its builders ever imagined.

Penryn must surely be England's 'Granite Borough'. For well over 200 years quarrying from the high ground of Carnmenellis to the west has been one of its mainstays. One of the great problems was transporting such a heavy material from the quarries of Mabe, Constantine and Stithians parishes to the coast for shipment and the picture above shows a block of dressed granite being carried by four-horse traction on one of the specially built wagons across Penryn bridge, probably to be loaded at Freeman's wharf.

This is probably Polkanuggo quarry, one of more than seventy quarries in the granite country behind the town, in 1895, soon after Freeman's had introduced steam traction engines for use towing carts and for lifting the blocks on and off the carts. Nineteen quarry workers pose for the camera, including the quarry manager, wearing bow tie and bowler hat, and two engineers on the engine.

Granite from Penryn has been used throughout the world. As early as 1819 the MP for the borough, Mr Swann, who had bought his way into Parliament by bribing voters, was made chairman of the committee for the erection of Waterloo Bridge and he ensured that the granite came from the quarries of Mabe and Stithians and was exported through Penryn for which harbour dues were payable to the mayor. He was later imprisoned for bribery. The picture above shows a 40-ton block from the Mabe quarries being transported to Penryn railway station using two traction engines.

Traction engines were adopted by Freeman's in the 1880s. Accidents were common between the quarries and the port, especially on the very steep hills into the town. An engine has come to grief at Hillhead, just below the railway bridge, probably as a result of brake failure. After water and sewer pipes were laid in the town loads such as this frequently crushed the pipes, giving rise to regular complaints from the Town Council. Freeman's traction engines were eventually replaced, firstly by steam and then by motor lorries in the 1920s.

The Penryn granite industry was dominated by the Freeman family until 1936 when the company became Freeman and McLeod. The Freeman yard was set up on the south shore of the river, originally on both sides of the bridge, in 1848 and a granite wall was built along the entire frontage. By 1868 it covered three acres of creekside land. The sheds accommodated over 100 masons and four cranes were kept busy loading ships such as these seen here alongside the yard. The schooner and steamship above lie against the wharves where the depth of water varied according to the degree of dredging carried out by the Town Council, who were constantly criticized for their neglect of this essential service. The ketch *Emma*, below, (last seen in the Town Quay basin at Falmouth on p. 95) is overshadowed by the gantry which dominated the yard and one of the loading cranes which still survives despite the almost total disappearance of all other traces of the industry. There were disasters to granite-carrying vessels from Penryn, such as that in November 1891 when the cargo of *Elizabeth*, a Cardigan-based ketch of 36 tons carrying 50 tons of granite for the Devonport dockyard extension, shifted in heavy sea and the ship foundered off Rame Head near the entrance to Plymouth Sound. The post-war decline in the use of natural stone and its replacement by cheaper cement and imported Norwegian granite led to the closure of the yard in 1965.

The Freeman yard took granite from its many quarries to be finished alongside the Penryn river from which vast quantities of stone were exported. Originally, all work was done by hand, and as early as 1861 over a hundred masons were employed in the yard, mainly on architectural and monumental work as most of the work on large engineering contracts was done in the quarries. By 1911 the number had risen to nearer 200, probably because less of this sort of work was being done in the quarries but concentrated where mechanical equipment could be used. Machine operators were becoming as important as the masons as mechanization was introduced for purposes such as cutting, smoothing, polishing and turning on an enormous lathe. The picture here shows equipment for smoothing the granite driven by compressed air from the pipes at each position. Granite was worked in two rows of open-fronted sheds, facing each other, and towards the bridge there was a large, covered granite building known as the pattern shop where templates were produced for shaping the stone for major engineering works. The yard was by far the largest in the south-west and in addition to the contracts mentioned overleaf, architectural work was executed for many London buildings including the British Museum, the Esso building, London University, the National Gallery, Scotland Yard and the Old Bailey, as well as both Liverpool Cathedrals, the National Library and the University of Wales in Aberystwyth and the National Museum of Wales in Cardiff. Monuments were a speciality of the yard and particular pride was taken in works such as the Albert Memorial, the Naval Monument at Greenwich, Westminster Cathedral and, more recently, the much-publicized Taylor-Woodrow sculpture named 'Teamwork' in Ealing.

Major engineering works all over the world have been constructed using Cornish granite and much of this has come from the Penryn yard. Among them are the breakwaters at Alderney, Dover and Portland, the Manchester Ship Canal, docks at Singapore, Buenos Aires, Bombay, Famagusta, Gibraltar, Colombo, Malta, Hull, Birkenhead, Cardiff, Liverpool, London and Chatham. In 1868 forts were built at Plymouth, Spithead, and in the Thames estuary, and some were still in use in the Second World War as anti-aircraft defences. Many of the country's lighthouses were made here, including those in the Channel Isles, Dover, Folkestone and Tynemouth. Around the Cornish coast the first Bishop's Rock light, the second on the Longships, and the Wolf Rock were all products of the Penryn masons and, in the picture above, the Fastnet lighthouse is taking shape. Carefully numbered, interlocking blocks are assembled, dry set, layer by layer, in the form of a large three-dimensional jigsaw puzzle. This particular contract, executed between 1899 and 1903 and eventually assembled on the rock ten miles off the south coast of Ireland, involved 70,000 cubic feet of granite, mostly from the huge Carnsew Quarry, near Mabe Burnthouse. Great accuracy in shaping the granite blocks was necessary. The erection of a lighthouse on site could be a hazardous operation especially on isolated, exposed rocks such as the Longships, Wolf and Bishop's Rock. While building the Wolf Rock lighthouse over the eight years up to 1869 it was only possible for the workmen to land on 266 occasions – an average of 33 per year – and the stone had to be carried to the rock from a workyard in Penzance, seventeen miles away, on the site of the present Trinity House Museum.

Freeman's were not the only granite merchants in Penryn. At various times W. Hosken and Co. had a yard and quay in Commercial Road but they ceased trading in 1910 because of competition; the West of England Granite Company of Diplock's Quay (adjacent to the Freeman yard) was taken over in 1892, and at the top of the town C.W. Andrew (above) was a stone and monumental mason with a work force of twenty-one men when this photograph was taken.

Labour relations in the granite industry were consistently good, and three generations of the Freeman family established a reputation for fair dealing. But strikes did occur for a number of reasons, mainly related to pay, and a fourteen week strike in 1929, when workmen asked for an increase of 2d. per hour, was eventually settled 'by an increase of $\frac{1}{2}$d. an hour for mechanics and 75% of that sum to quarrymen' only because of the fear that a £600,000 order for stone for Lambeth Bridge might be lost, with serious consequences to the Cornish granite trade. This picture shows workmen waiting outside Penryn Town Hall during one of these disputes.

Quay Hill has changed out of all recognition since 1954 when this photograph, above, was taken. In 1893 there were two inns: the Anchor, the sign on the left side of the road, and the Swan. The Church Institute was further up on the right, and on the left were the offices of the West of England Bone and Manure Company (p. 135) whose buildings stretched southwards to the Budock creek. Another business, established in Market Street in 1863 by Mr S. Cox, son of one of the founders of the Falmouth shipbuilders, was Cox and Son, ironmongers and oil importers, which moved to larger premises in Quay Hill in 1880 on the near side of the large building above and shown in greater detail below in the 1930s. After a move to new premises adjacent to the bridge in 1934, the business finally closed in 1969.

Quay Hill curves upwards past the Square, some houses in which date from the early eighteenth century but seen here about 1908 with Bolitho's butchery van making its deliveries. There is a story that the earliest houses in the Square did not continue the line of those in Broad Street because a large, venerable elm tree grew there causing the houses to be set back. Back to back with these houses was The Green, an east-facing open space dating back many centuries in the borough's history and frequently mentioned in its records. On 13 May 1941 enemy aircraft dropped bombs in this area which demolished the houses seen here behind the butcher's van, the Green and Quay Hill. Eighteen people were killed, ranging from 2-year-old Ronald Pascoe, of 3 Quay Hill, to 78-year-old John Rapson, of 3 The Green, and the area now forms a Garden of Remembrance.

Some of the borough's most impressive buildings are seen here on the right side of Broad Street, once known as Our Lady Street. They belonged originally to the merchants whose gardens stretched down to the shore of St Gluvias creek; those on the other side were less opulent as their gardens did not extend down to the Budock creek – the working class Bohill area intervened. The post office, extreme right, was opened in July 1905, but the building has been altered to shop fronts since the post office moved to the upper part of the town.

This view of Broad Street from its western end shows, in the immediate foreground, the Fish Cross, the former fish market which the *Penryn Advertiser* reported that the Corporation was about to demolish, in January 1894, as revenue from it was almost nil, adding 'the cross will look naked and strange without its market with its cross in front and those who stand on street corners will miss a place of shelter'. As the crest on its upper floor suggests, the building on the right is the old fire station, built 1899, and the tall, three-storey house next but one to it is one of several attractive old houses at this end of the street, one of whose occupants in the 1790s was Falmouth Packet captain, Robert Dillon, who may have rebuilt it as it is today. On the left is the pillared entrance of Chapman's Hotel, now the King's Arms, in front of which stands the Globe horse bus, which ran a regular service between Penryn and Falmouth until replaced by motor buses in the 1920s. The bus also ran excursions, as this extract from the *Penryn Advertiser* of 7 August 1886 shows: although residents at the western end of the town would no doubt travel to the Falmouth beaches by train, the bus departing from the Fish Cross would save the residents at this end of the town the tiresome climb up to the station. The gardens of the houses on the left originally ran down to the St Gluvias creek and, in her fascinating *Penryn in the Eighteenth Century*, June Palmer quotes some of the deeds of properties here as having 'an orchard adjacent to the sea . . . lately converted to a deal yard', 'a quay with liberty to land and ship salt fish', and others had fish cellars, warehouses and yards at the end of the garden.

Horse buses were replaced by motor vehicles in the early 1920s, and in both pictures a 40 hp Lacre charabanc (so named as each row of seats was entered by its own separate door) stands outside Falmouth's Greenbank Hotel. Journeys could not have been very comfortable, especially in bad weather, as the only protection for passengers at the end of each 'bench' was a canvas blind, seen here rolled up, while the solid tyres ensured a bumpy ride on the roads of the day. The absence of windscreen wipers may explain why the driver preferred to keep the windscreen partly open and a close inspection of the name boards erected by the Penryn and Falmouth Motor Company shows that local rivalry is appeased by having on one side 'Penryn and Falmouth' and on the other 'Falmouth and Penryn'. As time went on more bus companies ran on this local service so that by 1927, sixty-nine journeys ran daily. In October 1930 the *Penryn Advertiser* published regular complaints of obstruction in the town's narrow streets.

In 1802 Robert Southey, Poet Laureate, having landed in Falmouth from a Packet, was travelling by coach to London and said of Penryn, 'The ill-built and narrow streets seem to have been contrived to make as many acute angles in the road and take the traveller up and down as many steep declivities as possible.' Part of this journey would have taken him along the streets shown here as the route through Penryn in those days was via St Thomas's Street, Lower Market Street, down either St Gluvias Street or Truro Lane to the Praze, then up Truro Hill. Less than a century later, probably in the 1880s, the view is dominated by the Town Hall and Market House which divides the main street as it runs along the crest of the steep-sided spur of land which separates the port's two creeks. This prominent building was not, as was once thought, built on the site of St Mary's chapel, which seems to have been located at the top of St Thomas's Street. Dating from some time in the sixteenth century, it was the focus of the town's commercial, administrative and corrective affairs (the prison was there, too), but the clock tower which dominates the scene was not built until 1839, and the illuminated clock faces added in November 1909 in memory of Mr G.A. Jenkins, town clerk for forty-eight years. On the upper side, in deep shadow in this midday photograph, is, first, the Terrace of largely residential properties on its high pavement with the more opulent houses of Upper Market Street running down past the Town Hall. Immediately to the right of the clock tower several buildings have since been demolished, first to build the Wesley chapel (p. 149) in 1893 and later, in 1954, to make Saracen Place. On the left the more commercial side is made up of Lower Street, then Lower Market Street, the division being at the left of the clock tower where St Gluvias Street, the original way to the church, goes off steeply to the bridge across the head of the creek. Near the end of this street, the gable-end is that of the Teetotal or Rechabite Hall, built in 1852 and used regularly for town meetings. The Elephant and Castle Hotel was one of the Borough's principal hostelries and advertised regularly in the *Penryn Advertiser* as a 'Posting Establishment'.

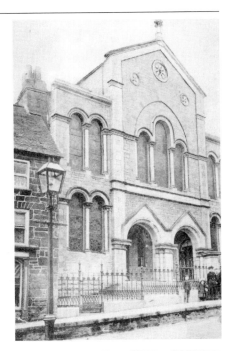

This impressive Wesleyan chapel was opened on 14 February 1893, before which its site had been occupied by the houses seen opposite, dating back to the eighteenth century. The chapel is a fine example of a typical Nonconformist building of the time with an excellent plastered ceiling and gallery round three sides. The house shown next door was occupied in the late eighteenth century by Jonathan Hornblower, a member of the famous Cornish engineering family whose grave in St Gluvias churchyard has recently been found. It was demolished in the 1950s to give access to the more modern part of the town via Saracen Place.

This sixty-year-old view of the lower convergence of the two streets shows the trend of many old town centres, where formerly residential properties have had their ground floors converted for retail purposes while the upper storeys, which are rarely given a second glance, remain largely unchanged. The projecting windows halfway down on the right denote the location of an inn named the King's Arms long before that name was transferred to the hotel in the distance with the pillared entrance. Throughout the eighteenth and much of the nineteenth centuries the houses belonged to rich and influential members of the borough community.

Descending from the Fish Cross
(p. 146) to the earliest crossing of the
College river on the road to Falmouth
is St Thomas's Street, its name main-
taining the direct link with nearby
Glasney. The houses on the left have
been meticulously preserved as a result
of the work of the Penryn Buildings
Survey Group. Behind these properties
once stood Glasney College, and built
into one of them is a pair of granite pillars reputed to have been one of its
entrances named 'College Ope'. On the
right, where once stood Queen Anne
Cottage, the story is one of almost total
destruction in the interests of road
widening and modern housing. After
the Dissolution this became the industrial area of the town with fish cellars,
a tannery, timber imports, boat building, flour merchants, a woollen mill
and several malthouses, mostly with
their private quays on the north side of
the Budock creek.

This reminder of Penryn's early water
supply stands in a small enclosure near
the bottom of St Thomas's Street. It was
only after James Blatch Cox had laid on
water to Falmouth from reservoirs in
the College valley in 1847 that Penryn
had access to a regular supply but there
were frequent complaints and disagree-
ments, mainly over cost and regularity
of supply, and in March 1874 Falmouth
Waterworks Company advertised to the
effect that all public taps would be cut
off on 3 March and that any individuals
wishing to have a piped supply should
contact the company. Throughout the
later nineteenth century there were frequent observations that a water cart was
required to keep down dust in the
streets.

Little Falmouth lies in a small creek a short distance north of Flushing and has long been notable as an industrial site. As early as the sixteenth century a thriving business existed exporting pilchards to Europe, and by the mid-seventeenth century Richard Lobb, an influential Parliamentarian who prospered during the Civil War and Interregnum, had established a 'Pilchard Palace' which processed fish for export. A century later a small village had grown up with a lime kiln, a timber yard and the Symonds shipyard where several Falmouth Packet vessels were built. To facilitate ship repairing, Symonds built the first graving (dry) dock in the estuary in 1820, the walls of which may still be seen clearly. After 1851 John Trethowan, who had another yard on the Bar, took over and built such well known vessels as *Charlotte Padbury*, a barque for the West Australian trade and probably the largest wooden vessel to have been built in Cornwall. The picture below shows a group of workers building a large boat in the Trethowan yard. During and after the Second World War Falmouth Boat Construction Company have run the yard as a boat repair facility, their reputation shown by the regular appearance in their sheds of the lifeboats of the RNLI.

The village of Flushing, reputedly named by or after the Dutch engineers from Vlissingen who reclaimed the marsh at the mouth of the Kersey valley (above, extreme left) and built sea walls at the northern end of the present village, extends nearly half a mile along the waterfront on the eastern shore of the Penryn river. The ferry quay (left), shown in close-up below with its characteristic dry-stone construction, is crowded with spectators watching the race between the quay punts ICU (dark hull) and *Cobweb* in the centre foreground. Behind the houses on the ferry quay may be seen the roof of the four-storey Great Cellars, built soon after 1700 to store goods carried as unofficial cargo on the Falmouth Packets. At the right end of these houses is a narrow alley known as Barky's Ope, still cobbled in the way that all village streets once were. The low waterside building is the Salt Water Baths constructed after the Prince Regent had made such bathing fashionable in the early nineteenth century. New quay, on the extreme right, built to protect the village and its boats from south-easterly gales, is backed by New Quay House, one of the village's most historic buildings, dating from about 1700 and once used as a warehouse for the storage of Packet goods and, later, by Jonathan Mayne as a bakery in the 1830s.

On the ferry quay stand several large granite bollards used at one time to moor large vessels such as the Packet brigs. The glass-fronted conservatory-like structure on the right is the Watermen's Rest, built in the 1880s at the behest of Mrs Punnet as a shelter in bad weather for the men who operated the small boats which acted as the harbour's taxi service, carrying people and goods to and from ships in the harbour. Upstairs in the building behind it was a Mission Room set up by Mrs Punnet's brother, Revd Adoniah Sutton, vicar of Penwerris. To its left is a small granite arch and doorway, dated 1822, which was once used as a source of water for replenishing ships before a voyage; as a Packet on the South American station required over 4,000 gallons loading must have been an arduous task, made easier if the vessel was able to come alongside the quay at high tide.

To the north of this quay is the older part of the village where the yards of the smaller houses have easy access to tidal water. Behind the two gentlemen on the seat was at one time a cowshed from which milk was sold to villagers; the adjoining house is Ferry Cottage. In a house along the waterfront here lived James Silk Buckingham, one of several Flushing men to attain high rank in the Royal Navy – his autobiography gives a fascinating insight into life in the village and at sea in the early years of the nineteenth century.

The earliest Flushing ferry was incorporated into the Falmouth Charter of 1661 when Charles II gave Sir Peter Killigrew the right to run a ferry, probably from Smithick to the quay at Flushing. Since then many ferries have operated across this stretch of water and there have been several disputes relating to the ferry lease. In 1887 John Mead used open boats from Greenbank until the steamer *Greyhound* (see *Falmouth* p. 112) arrived in 1888, for which the Sara foundry of Penryn installed a new engine. By this time the Falmouth end of the ferry had been moved to the Market Strand Pier and, above, *Greyhound* is seen alongside the newly constructed granite jetty. After 1900 the service was taken over by *Lily* and, later, in 1914, by the motor vessel *Miranda* (below) which used to operate from 6 a.m. to midnight, fares 'single ½d., return 1d., monthly tickets available', until replaced by *Miranda II* in 1934.

The oyster fishery at Flushing had been a largely domestic operation until the early nineteenth century when a series of severe winters on the east coast threatened their survival and large stocks were brought down and laid in the Fal, Helford and Penryn rivers. Several Essex families settled in the village. Philip Hill, a Freeman of Colchester who owned the Globe and Ship Inns in the village, was killed in 1869 when he fell off the quay at Flushing, soon after his daughter, Kate, had married a schoolmaster from the training ship *Ganges* while only 14 years old when her parents were away and the vicar's deputy unaware of her true age. Another casualty is shown in the picture above. The inscription on the tombstone reads: 'To the memory of Mr John Varral, aged 49 years, Master of the Smack *Ebenezer* of Rochester, Kent, who was unfortunately killed by falling down her hold whilst unballasting at Flushing port, Falmouth, April 7th, 1846.' The photograph of his tombstone was taken in Mylor churchyard by the Falmouth photographers, Truscott Bros, of 13 Berkeley Place, for his family in Rochester; it now forms part of the paving in the south aisle of Mylor church.

The small inlet towards the northern end of the village is the Fish Cross, the original mouth of the Kersey stream. On the quay to the right the local fishermen displayed their catch for sale. The building on the right is the original Seven Stars Inn, its signboard over the door. It was here, in 1810, that the so-called Packet mutineers met to plan their strategy while the authorities rowed from Falmouth to Mylor church and approached overland in the vain hope of catching them unawares. The three-storey building next door was at one time a lodging house for sailors at a time when accommodation on ships was very poor and, when in harbour, some of the crew tasted the comparative luxury of life ashore. The lower photograph shows the head of the Fish Cross with a view along the narrow Trefusis Street, once Market Street, with shops and houses on both sides as the road curves away towards the quay. The large group of children may have been the pupils of the local school in Coventry Street.

Much of the older part of Flushing near the Fish Cross is below the level of a very high spring tide and at one time, before the level of the roads was raised slightly in 1950 when mains water was brought to the village, floods such as that shown here were common in the lower parts of Coventry Street and Trefusis Street. It is likely that the original course of the Kersey stream roughly followed this section of road and, as it was the lowest point, water from the Fish Cross would flow up here and subside only on the falling tide. The village school, built on land given by Lord Clinton in 1895, is at the far end of this road, as the road sign suggests, at a part of the valley known, significantly, as the Sands. Children had sometimes to be rowed part of the way to school. On the left is the side wall of the Seven Stars while, at the far end, Coventry Street, once Moor Street, curves to the left and rises slightly past the former Custom House to meet Kersey Road which runs as a cul-de-sac to the upper end of what is now called Orchard Vale (see p. 158).

Orchard Vale, forming the upper part of the Kersey valley, is now covered with post-war housing but was once a country lane leading up to fields near the entrance to the Trefusis estate.

A group of village lads outside the Standard Hotel. The houses above the hotel in St Peter's Terrace, once New Road, have been the homes of many notable people since the 1780s, especially those associated with the Packet Service. Capt. John Bull lived at No. 8, just past the spectacular monkey-puzzle tree, with his first wife before he moved to the much grander Marlborough Cottage on the outskirts of Falmouth about 1810. His neighbours were members of the Sulivan family, several of whom became admirals. Further up lived Edward Pellew who, as a junior Naval officer, preferred a crew of Cornish miners to pressed men and became a hero by capturing the first French prize during the Napoleonic Wars in 1793. At the top of the hill is St Peter's church, built in 1842 to save the villagers the long walk to Mylor church, partly with money left by another packet captain, Adoniah Schuyler, an American Colonial and Naval Officer who remained loyal to the Crown after Independence and joined the Packet Service.

The Trefusis family has retained ownership of much of the promontory between Carrick Roads and the Penryn river for over 800 years and the present house, seen above, built in 1890, is the third on the site. Samuel Trefusis was instrumental in trying to move the headquarters of the Packet Service to Flushing in the early eighteenth century, using the influence obtained by marrying the daughters of two Postmasters General – one after the other. Attempts have been made on at least two occasions to link both sides of the Penryn river with a bridge or causeway, and in 1859–60 plans were made to build a town to rival Falmouth on the south-facing slopes of Trefusis Point.

Kiln Quay on the extreme right is named from a former nearby lime kiln, one of several around the estuary which used limestone imported from south Devon to 'sweeten' the acidic Cornish soil and for building purposes. The houses shown here were built by Dr Crossman early in this century, the lower one as a dwelling for himself on the site of the former Shepherd's House, below which Richard Tregenza had a boat-building shed, and the larger one, Glensilva, as a nursing home at a time when Flushing was developing a reputation as a health resort.

Acknowledgements

This book is really a sequel to *Falmouth in Old Photographs* published about two years ago. There were so many good photographs which had to be omitted from that volume and so many people who had read it urged me to write another that *The Fal Estuary* had to be written. After collecting photographs and information for over a year, however, there were too many for one book and it was decided to divide the estuary along the same line that the Falmouth and Truro Corporations had agreed to use nearly three centuries ago. Many people have rendered assistance in a variety of ways and I thank them all, but most especially my gratitude for special help must go to:

Louie and Bert Kendall • Jean and Len Prynn • Sheila and John Tregay
Len Ainslee • Peter Ball • David Barnicoat • Jim Benney • Andy Campbell
Edgar Davies • Jimmy Green • Keith Hancock • Lennox Hold • Patrick Johns
Derek Kitto • Gordon Martin • Maurice Osborne • Bob Paterson
Roger Penhalurick • Norman Selwood • Bert Thomas • Nicholas Trefusis
• Gerald Trethowan • Mary Canan • Janet Heard • Jane Jackson
Mary Keppel • Phyllis Mehaffey • Margaret Morris • Lady Ursula Redwood
Margaret Ross • Ida Williams

As well as being my sternest critic and adviser, my wife has continued to show patience and understanding well beyond the limit of normal domestic tolerance. Simon Thraves has solved my problems with his customary blend of tact and composure. The next volume is already in its formative stage and should, if all goes according to plan, be ready in about a year. I look forward to the expeditions by land and water its preparation will entail.